The

Vera O'Toole is alone, adrift and living dang... New York where she survives as a call-girl. But she has a sustaining thought, a dream. She is not alone, she feels, because she has a family in Ireland; she belongs; indeed, some day she may even become worthy of that family. Now, as the story begins, she returns home to Ireland to pay her respects to her dead and beloved grandmother and to discover her dream, her sustaining thought, turning into a nightmare . . .

Tom Murphy's work includes *A Whistle in the Dark* (1961), *On the Outside* (1962), *A Crucial Week in the Life of a Grocer's Assistant* (1966), *Famine*, *The Orphans* (both 1968), *The Morning After Optimism* (1971), *The White House* (1972), *On the Inside* (1974), *The Sanctuary Lamp* (1975), *The J. Arthur Maginnis Story* (1976), *Epitaph Under Ether* (1979), *The Blue Macushla* (1980), *The Informer* (adaptation, 1981), *Conversations on a Homecoming*, *The Gigli Concert* (both 1983), *The Seduction of Morality* (novel, 1984), *Bailegangaire* (1985), *Too Late for Logic* (1989), *The Patriot Game* (1991), *She Stoops to Folly* (adaptation, 1995) and *The Wake* (1998). He was born in Tuam, County Galway. He lives in Dublin and is a member of Aosdána and the Irish Academy of Letters.

for a complete catalogue of Methuen Drama write to:

Methuen
Random House
20 Vauxhall Bridge Road
London SW1V 2SA

Tom Murphy

The Wake

Methuen Drama

Copyright © 1998 by Tom Murphy
The right of Tom Murphy to be identified as the author of this
work has been asserted by him in accordance with the
Copyright, Designs and Patents Act, 1988

First published in Great Britain in 1998
by Methuen
Random House, 20 Vauxhall Bridge Road, London SW1V 2SA

Random House Australia (Pty) Limited
20 Alfred Street, Milsons Point, Sydney, New South Wales 2061, Australia

Random House New Zealand Limited
18 Poland Road, Glenfield, Auckland 10, New Zealand

Random House South Africa (Pty) Limited
Endulini, 5A Jubilee Road, Parktown 2193, South Africa

Random House UK Limited Reg. No. 954009

A CIP catalogue record for this book is available from the British Library

Papers used by Random House UK Limited are natural, recyclable products
made from wood grown in sustainable forests. The manufacturing processes
conform to the environmental regulations of the country of origin.

ISBN 0 413 71410 1

Typeset by Deltatype Ltd, Birkenhead, Merseyside
Printed and bound in Great Britain by Cox & Wyman Ltd, Reading,
Berkshire

Caution

à
mon agent provocateur extraordinaire
alexandra cann

The Wake was first performed at the Abbey Theatre, Dublin, on 28 January 1998. The cast was as follows:

Vera	Jane Brennan
Mrs Conneeley	Pat Leavy
Finbar	David Herlihy
Henry	Stanley Townsend
Marcia	Anna Healy
Mary Jane	Olwen Fouere
Tom	Phelim Drew
Caitriona	Jennifer O'Dea
Father Billy	Seán Rocks
Norman	Simon Jewell/Brian Martin

Director Patrick Mason
Set Designer Francis O'Connor
Costume Designer Joan O'Clery
Music Conor Linehan
Lighting Ben Ormerod
Sound Dave Nolan
Stage Director Colette Morris

Scene One

An open space: the country. Night.

Off, in the distance, a light. The purr of an engine, a car. It stops. The engine is switched off, then the lights.

And **Vera** *comes in, as one might to an empty church, warily. To stop, hold her breath, as if listening. Now she moves about silently. She comes to a stop, fixing on a memory of something or someone. A sigh overtakes her, she catches it back, holds it. And now releases it, her face moving into a smile of acceptance.*

She's thirty-seven. (Ideally, she is a large, handsome woman.) Urban dress: a wig, a mackintosh coat hangs open over a tan, suede suit; the skirt is a bit short . . . perhaps she hasn't quite got the hang of dress.

There is someone approaching. Not knowing what else to do, **Vera** *moves into the shadows.*

And **Mrs Conneeley** *arrives. She is unsure whether to stop or pass by . . .*

Mrs Conneeley *is in her sixties. A country woman. She is holding her long, unbuttoned coat about her; a long, man's type of coat. She is an unassuming woman; she has a lot of integrity, a lot of what used to be called 'nature'.*

Mrs Conneeley . . . Is it Vera?

Vera . . . Mrs Conneeley?

Mrs Conneeley Is it Vera? . . . D'you know we were saying it might be you – Aw, is it Vera! Paddy was above with the sheep while ago and saw the car, so I came over just in case. How are you, how are you!

Vera Mrs Conneeley.

Mrs Conneeley How are you? (*Her two hands are on top of* **Vera***'s.*)

Vera Fine.

Mrs Conneeley You came home to pay your respects.

Vera   I did.

Mrs Conneeley   You did. Your poor grandmother. I wish we were meeting under different circumstances. Poor Winnie.

Vera   When I got the news I came home as quickly as I could arrange things. I! (*She flaps her hands to her sides, awkwardly.*)

Mrs Conneeley   I understand. But d'you know I'm so pleased to see you. And how are they all in town, your family?

Vera   Oh, they're all – I haven't seen them yet! They don't know I'm coming.

Mrs Conneeley   You didn't tell them!

Vera   No! Faster than a letter just to arrive.

Mrs Conneeley   That's going to be a great surprise for them.

Vera   It is.

Mrs Conneeley   'Tis. You'll come over for a cup of tea? No! – No now! No, you will! No! No!

Vera *laughs, responding to the warmth of the invitation.*

Mrs Conneeley   Leave – leave the car.

Vera   The air here!

Mrs Conneeley   Yes.

They are moving off together.

Vera   And I have another niece.

Mrs Conneeley   You have. And what's her name?

Vera   Carol.

Mrs Conneeley   That's a nice name . . .

Scene Two

Mrs Conneeley's *house: two chairs and a cooker.*

Vera *and* **Mrs Conneeley** *are coming in. (They have two cups of tea – this to avoid the fuss/business of making tea during the scene.) They are still in their overcoats.* **Vera** *is intoxicated by* **Mrs Conneeley**'s *warmth, house, conversation. And* **Mrs Conneeley** *is no less pleased with* **Vera**'s *company.*

Vera   They're good to me in all sorts of ways.

Mrs Conneeley   They send you all the news.

Vera   They're great like that. The house is lovely.

Mrs Conneeley   It's not bad – Oh, give me your coat, you'll be cold when you go out! Paddy and Julia are here with me. They're gone up to make the last hour in Melody's for a drink. Julia, his wife, she's nice. One of the Tierneys below? (*Meaning: 'Do you remember the Tierneys'?*) I've four grandchildren sleeping in there so I haven't many complaints in her. (*Going out with the coats:*) You're staying in the hotel?

Vera (*calls*)   It's closed down! They recommended that I sell it – (*Which, privately, casually, she finds odd, and she shrugs to herself.*) – and they're auctioning it for me.

Mrs Conneeley (*returning*)   I didn't know that – pull down to the fire. Fire? I miss the open hearth, d'you know, but if you open the door to the grate on this gazebo you at least have a place to spit.

Vera   And your other son?

Mrs Conneeley   Francis?

Vera   Francis.

Mrs Conneeley   Isn't he a solicitor. . . ? (*She is surprised and a little amused at Francis's success: what does* **Vera** *think of it.*)

Vera's *face expresses appreciation.*

Mrs Conneeley   He's married too sure and has a practice in Newcastle.

Vera   Mmm!

Mrs Conneeley   And yourself?

Vera   Oh!

Mrs Conneeley   You haven't found him yet.

Vera   Well, *some* relationships.

Mrs Conneeley   Yes?

Vera   I'm all right the way I am.

Mrs Conneeley   Indeed and maybe you are and as well off! New York you're in all the time?

Vera   Yes.

Mrs Conneeley   Hah?

Vera   Mainly.

Mrs Conneeley   Now. And you're doing well?

Vera   Quite well.

Mrs Conneeley   Yes?

Vera   Oh! – 'I've been a rover'.

Mrs Conneeley (*laughing*)   Yes! – 'I've been a rover'.

Vera   Still looking for myself.

Mrs Conneeley   You are! 'I've been a rover.' I know. Lord, she was a powerful strong woman in her time. Mighty. (*She smiles shyly.*) She was very fond of you.

Vera *smiles*.

Mrs Conneeley   You were a long time living with her.

Vera   Eleven years.

Mrs Conneeley   Eleven. Now. And she was lonely for you when they took you home again.

Vera   I was lonely for her too. But I used to – long – to be with my family.

Mrs Conneeley   I know.

Vera   My brother and sisters.

Mrs Conneeley   I understand.

Vera   I used to – wonder – what had I done wrong for them to send me out here to live with grandma.

Mrs Conneeley   It's a strange thing, isn't it? Loneliness. (*And she begins to laugh at loneliness:*) Well, isn't it? What does it mean? Sometimes, d'you know, I think about it and I have to laugh. What!? Married or single or widowed or as children – or married six times over maybe! – it's all the same, that's the way we are.

They smile at each other.

Mrs Conneeley   What'll we talk about next? (*Appreciatively; the cooker again:*) It makes great bread though. Paddy and Julia I know want me to sign this place over to them, but what's the hurry on them. I'm not dead yet. Well, I'm so pleased to see you.

They smile at each other.

Oh, and she could be cross?

Vera (*laughs*)   She could.

Mrs Conneeley   She had her ways. And not much loss in her, mind you, towards the end. The sight was what troubled her most. Oh now, when the sight begins to go, Vera. And you're not unlike her, God bless you: I can see the resemblance.

Vera   What age did they put on the coffin?

Mrs Conneeley   We were talking about that all right. Eighty-six?

Vera   . . . Yes. That would be about right. She told me she was born . . . (**Vera** *smiles:*) About a half a dozen years after the century, she said.

Mrs Conneeley   That'd be about right then. Eighty-six. (*And they are pleased that no mistake was made on the breastplate of the coffin.*) . . . And sure you must be . . . Thirty-four?

Vera   The last time I saw thirty-four, Mrs Conneeley, was on top of a bus.

And they laugh at age until **Mrs Conneeley**, *remembering her grandchildren, puts a finger to her lips.*

What day did she die?

Mrs Conneeley   What *day*? . . . Was it about the middle of February?

Vera   *Feb*ruary?

A dream is about to move into a nightmare.

Mrs Conneeley   Hah? . . . It's a terrible month for death.

Vera   I had thought . . .

Mrs Conneeley   . . . We thought all right when you weren't home for the funeral that maybe they forgot to tell you.

Vera   No! They write, they – We've been in constant touch – Well, about the hotel, the – Other matters. (*Smiles:*) It slipped their minds.

But **Mrs Conneeley** *has begun to smile painfully.*

Mrs Conneeley   . . . And sure she'd have lasted another ten years.

The smile closing on **Vera**'s *face.*

Aw, God, Vera.

Vera's *waiting apprehension.*

Mrs Conneeley   Sure she'd have lasted another ten years if someone got to her . . . (*She is waiting for permission to continue.*) I'd be ashamed if people were to think us bad neighbours.

Vera *nods, or half nods, slowly.*

Mrs Conneeley She was very strong d'you know. But I knew for a good while the sight was going. You'd know it the way she wouldn't recognise you sometimes 'til you spoke. And I started to go over to see her? And tell Paddy, any time he was passing, to call in. Or I'd bring her over the drop of soup or whatever was going in the saucepan. That way. Because she was good. And I know well about that. And Paddy'd go over to give her the lift in the car to Mass of a Sunday, and home again afterwards. Or at least he'd ask, because sometimes she liked the walk. Or to take her to the village for her pension of a Friday. And the few groceries. But your brother didn't like it. Tom. Oh, I don't know. Maybe, I suppose, he thought we were after the farm. It happens. Well, it's his now. He has it stocked these two months. (*To herself:*) Hah?

Vera, *waiting, holding her breath.*

Mrs Conneeley *has been painfully smiling the above: Now the smile dissolving and hardening into anger, to stare at* **Vera**, *as if* **Vera** *were the enemy.*

Mrs Conneeley But how much land does anyone need? I know how much land – *and* property – a person needs. How much land does your grandmother need now? Or the man who used to be my husband need? Or anyone else for that matter . . . (*The anger dissolves the way it came, until she becomes soft again. To herself:*) You wouldn't know what's wrong with people. Unless it's something greatly innocent. (*Smiles at* **Vera***:*) Hah? . . . But your brother came out one evening and one of your sisters was with him. Paddy was in with her. And your brother followed Paddy out as Paddy was leaving to come home. And he said to Paddy: I'm sure you have more things to be doing than visiting old women. And tell your mother the same, he said. What could we do? Paddy was shaking telling me. What could we do? . . . Poor Winnie.

Vera *nods.*

Mrs Conneeley I think it was a Wednesday and Paddy
came in. Julia was there, feeding the youngest. I don't see
any smoke he said coming from Winnie Lally's, did ye see
her at all since Sunday? We left Julia there and went over
the road the two of us. First, to pass by, then look in the
windows. But it was hard to see in, d'you know. And I
called out her name? And Paddy tried the door, but it was
bolted from inside. I don't care he said then and I nodded
to him to go ahead.

Mrs Conneeley *has begun to weep, silently.*

Vera, *increasingly, has become upright in her chair. Now she is
nodding, positively, to continue.*

Mrs Conneeley Oh she was dead. Oh she was dead,
Vera. (*Her mouth is dry: she is trying to swallow.*)

Vera, *bolt upright, waiting for her to continue.*

Mrs Conneeley . . . She'd fell. She was there for a few
days, d'you know. She'd fell into the fire. But she got out
of it. She got out of it someway, the creature, crawled. But
couldn't get up. What could we do?

*She continues to weep. She emits a single wail. One hand, now, is
covering her eyes, like a visor; the other is held out and back to*
Vera. **Vera** *takes the hand, holds it, absently. She is frowning-
smiling. She shakes her head to deny what she has heard; it won't go
away: the frown-smile keeps returning.*

Mrs Conneeley . . . You're staying where? In the hotel?

Vera Ahmmm . . .

Mrs Conneeley That place is yours, isn't it?

Vera It's, ahmmm, yes. It's closed down. It doesn't mean
anything to me. I have to, have to go now, the plane, get
away. (*She has risen. A vague movement/gesture for something – her
coat.*)

Mrs Conneeley Hah? Sure you can't! Drive all that way

is it back to Dublin again tonight? . . . Stay in the front
room. Do!

Vera   No, I'll . . . They're all I . . . No, thanks.

Mrs Conneeley *goes out for* **Vera**'s *coat.* **Vera**, *alone, does
not know what she is going to do, where she is going to go. A stifled
sob.*

Vera   They're all I have.

Mrs Conneeley *returns with* **Vera**'s *coat: did* **Vera** *say
something?* **Vera** *shakes her head.*

Mrs Conneeley   I'm sorry. (*Her two hands on top of*
Vera's.) But I'd be ashamed if people were to think us bad
neighbours.

Vera   There was no wake.

Mrs Conneeley   There was no wake. There was an
inquest.

Vera   Heigh-ho!

Mrs Conneeley   Will you call again before you go
back? . . .

She is showing **Vera** *out. The lights have faded to nothing.*

Scene Three

Someone lights a candle. **Finbar**. *He has just got out of bed.*

Finbar's *place: a single bed and a broken armchair. (Maybe, just
out of the light, some bentwood chairs and a bastard table – 'A
composite'.)*

Finbar *is forty-one, lives alone in squalor, a bachelor. A mess of
hang-ups to do with class and sex. He is a product of a culture.
(Lifted as a boy by 'the authorities' and put into care, brutalised
there and sexually abused by the Christian Brothers.) He sells second-
hand furniture and holy medals. 'Fuckin'!': a squeak, a nervous, vocal
tic. Quick flash-point. A frightened scavenger.*

Finbar (*to himself*) What, what, who, Jesus? (*Feeble call:*) Is there someone there? ... (*To himself:*) Half past one in the morning. (*Calls:*) Just a! (*Coughs.*) Just a, just a! (*He turns it into a bout of coughing. Calls:*) Just a minute! (*To himself:*) I'll have to go out. Will I? ... Fuckin'!

He pulls on his trousers, takes the candle and goes out to (what is meant to be) the front door.

Finbar (*en route or inside the front door*) Yes?

Vera *is outside, mackintosh over her arm, overnight bag beside her, smiling.*

Vera Hi!

Finbar Yes?

Vera Hi!

Finbar Who?

Vera Me! ... Vera!

Finbar (*to himself*) Vera? ... Vera. What are you doing here? (*He has 'opened the door'.*)

Vera Hi!

Finbar You put the!

Vera Can I come in?

Finbar Put the heart crossways in me!

Vera Can I come in?

Finbar ... Liberty Hall as the fella says. Watch your step. Wait'll I light the way. Stick close to the wall. My antiques. The lights are gone ... (*He has led her back to his room.*) Well! Well! This is a surprise! This is – how shall I put it? – a total surprise! Is that your car out there? – Sit down. And it was only the other day that I – No! sit on this: (*The bed.*) If you don't mind. The fuckin' springs are gone in that. And it was only the other – you'll excuse the French. And it was only the other day that I was thinking about you – You're welcome, sit down, you're welcome.

Vera Thanks.

Finbar What?

Vera Nothing.

Finbar The electricity. (*Is cut off.*)

Vera Romantic.

Finbar What?

Vera No! (*Meaning, 'it's fine'.*)

Finbar And I'm afraid it's the maid's day off.

Vera It's great! (*The room is great.*) Would you like a drink?

Finbar Now, that might not be!

The might not be a bad idea, and he goes out. Now that she is alone: her tired confusion and what on earth is she doing here.

Finbar (*off*) A social call?

Vera Yeh! . . . Is that okay?

Finbar . . . Only be a sec!

Vera No hurry!

She opens her jacket, the top button of her blouse, considers the next one down. She produces a bottle from her overnight bag. He returns with two wet glasses.

Finbar Here we are. Well! Well! What's new?

Vera Oh!

Finbar Not much. I didn't know you were home – Did you feel the touch of frost out there? – When did you arrive?

Vera Just now.

Finbar Just? Did you!

Vera Yeh. (*She is pouring the drinks.*)

Finbar Speak your word said the guard at the gate, yes

but bear it to Caesar straight!

Vera   Nice glasses.

Finbar   Now, they're special. They, would you believe, came out of a castle in Scotland.

Vera   Down the hatch!

Finbar   Down the!

They drink.

State of the place.

Vera   On the contrary.

Finbar   What?

Vera   On the contrary, Finbar.

Finbar (*nods. Then*)   And you only just arrived this minute?

Vera   Yeh.

Finbar   You came home for the auction, the hotel – saw the ad.

Vera   Yeh.

Finbar   Heard a good one. Fella goes into the doctor's yeh see and the doctor examines him anyway. I'm afraid says the doctor I've bad news for you, you've only three minutes to live, do you have a last request. And says your man: a soft-boiled egg? ... What?

Vera *starts laughing.*

Finbar   Jesus! Jesus! A soft-boiled egg!

Vera   I drove into town of course. You know? Driving round: Where *is* everyone? Where *is* the place? It's like a ghost town down there.

Finbar   Yeh?! Jesus, this's lovely, what is it?

Vera   Bourbon.

Finbar   You're not serious! Humphrey Bogart!

Vera Here's lookin' at you, kid!

Finbar And at you!

Vera Driving round the town: where will I go, where *can* I go? No place in my *own* home town to go to?! Had a bottle, didn't have a message, yeh? (*Then:*) Bingo! A name from the past, I thought what the hell, what the hell I thought, I'll try him, I'll *ask*, what can he do to you, the boy can only eat you for God's sake! I hope you don't mind?

Finbar No, I don't –

Vera I hope you don't mind, Finbar?

Finbar No, I –

Vera After all – Ah-haa! – that famous romance we had one time?

Finbar Oh yes! (*Though it is not at this stage the foremost memory in his mind.*)

Vera Wasn't that something – Wasn't-that-something! – Wasn't it, just!

Finbar Yeh.

Vera Ah-haa! How are you, Finbar?

Finbar Not a bother.

Vera You're okay?

Finbar Living it up – as you can see.

Vera You're okay?

Finbar You can't take it with you.

Vera You cannot take it with you, Finbar. And you can't come back for it either. (*Would he like his drink topped-up:*) Hmm?

Finbar I don't mind.

He draws his overcoat from among the bedclothes to drape it across his knees, to search the pockets.

Vera   Business?

Finbar   Would you like a gross or two of them glasses? Business, Vera? *Comme ci, comme ça*, up and down – Where did I leave them? Or a combination of canaries and stuffed parrots in a nice glass case? Can't find a fuckin' thing in the place since they cut me off. I'll do a deal for you. Yes, they cut the electricity on me. Oh, I'd pay them, no problem, *and* for the reconnection fee, but they're saying there's going to be a sudden general election and if that is to be the case, won't there be amnesties flying for everyone and anything from Mephisto O'Flynn our local politician. Where did I?

Vera   Cigarettes?

Finbar   D'you have some?

Vera   I have come prepared.

She is unzipping her overnight bag again, her head is down.
Finbar*'s misgivings/interest/calculation, watching her.*

Finbar   (*humourlessly*)   I must have left mine on the piano. Yes, I was thinking about you there lately.

Vera   Nothing good I hope, something bad I hope sincerely.

Finbar   No but, were you due another visit. We don't see you very often.

Vera   (*looks up: something childlike*)   But I think of here.

Finbar   What?

Vera   (*producing carton of cigarettes*)   Now we have all the essentials. Almost.

Finbar   Your mother's funeral, Lord have mercy on the soul of the woman, was the last time (*You were home.*), wasn't it?

Vera   There's been another death in the family since.

Finbar   They come in threes. Who?

Vera   My grandmother. (*She gives him a pack of cigarettes.*)

Finbar   Oh yes!

Vera   She damn near brought me up.

Finbar   Out the country. Thanks. (*For cigarettes.*) That was when we met: You weren't that long back in from the country.

Vera   Wasn't that something – Ah-haa! – when we met, wasn't it, just, Finbar!

Finbar   Jesus! (*And laughs: there is, now, a bitterness entering the memory.*)

Vera   (*childlike again for a moment*)   They say that I resemble her?

Finbar   Yeh? Jesus!

Vera   My grandmother. We shared the big bed – (*He is returning the pack of cigarettes to her:*) Keep them. Her bed. Sometimes I didn't have to go to school at all. 'Ah stay there, child, it's too cold to get up.' The two of us – I ask you! – my grandmother and myself, sitting up in bed for half the day – singing! (*Sings:*) 'Carry me back to ol'–' I ask you, Finbar, singing songs!

Finbar   Sorry to hear that.

Vera   For God's sake, eighty-six years of age – A good innings: Isn't that what you'd say yourself? – she's dead since February. (*She is searching for and finds her cigarette lighter:*) People used to say that she was cross: she *wasn't* cross: she was shy. (*Then, as she lights his cigarette:*) Can I stay?

Finbar   Thanks. (*For the light.*)

Vera   The hotel is closed down.

Finbar   'Tis.

Vera   Can I stay?

Finbar   ... Why?

Vera   I need to – Just somewhere to crash. For a few hours.

Finbar   Sleep?

Vera   Yeh. Whatever.

Finbar   Is this what you do in America?

Vera   Yeh! (*And laughs.*)

Finbar   (*laughs. Then*)   But! The place: chock-a-block. Furniture, my antiques – You saw them out there yourself: The hall, the! (*The rest of the house.*) They haven't been shifting too fast lately. So, there's only here. (*This room.*) And! (*Points:*) Backkitchen.

Vera   This is fine.

Finbar   A dealer – You would not believe it, Vera – can leave nothing outside his door any more. There's no respect left for law and order. Why should there be! The tinkers? – The rich are worse! – Pick up the papers! And there's only a few of them caught! And *they* get off! They're given presents of Mercs to get off in! And fuckin' quarter-million-pound handshakes! I think things have become so bad there's no one any more that knows how bad they are. So where do you go?

Vera   The rich will always be with us.

Finbar   What? ... They will! Can't leave a blessed, single, fuckin' thing out there! Well, at least nothing that's portable. Did you see anything in my garden as you were coming in that you could lift? You'd have to be a very strong man. No the only things I keep out there are heavy. That out there is my hernia department, rupture land, and let any or all enter it at their peril to test their strength. So, yeh see, chock-a-block. Nice lighter. (*He is toying with her lighter.*)

Vera   This is fine if it's all right with you.

Finbar (*shrugs that it's all right with him − but he won't say it*) . . . What would your family think, your brother say, your sisters?

Vera Who's to know?

Finbar Because − can I be frank? Though it's a well-known fact that these are not the Middle Ages, the authorities in this town can be very serious people. *I'm* the one they say is the danger, an enemy to their order? I'll tell you. Because, unlike my colleague in the antique business up the road there, John-John McNulty, who can say fuck them, *and mean it*, the reason why I say fuck them is because I'm frightened of every single one of them. D'you get my drift?

Vera D'you want me to leave?

Finbar Did *I*?! (*Did he say that.*) Would *I*?! . . . I'm only a simple man, that's all I'm saying. (*You.*) Can stay as long as you like as far as I'm concerned.

Vera (*a silent*) Thanks.

Finbar *shrugs 'Not at all'. He sips. He is still toying with her lighter. Now, a resentment is growing in him.*

Finbar That's settled then. Haven't a thing in my stomach. No but, what I was thinking back there was, you gave me one of these, one something like this one, one time.

Vera Did I?

Finbar You did.

Vera A lighter?

He nods.

You gave me a fountain pen.

Finbar I know I did. But!

She waits.

I know I did.

Vera (*it was*) A long time ago.

Finbar A long time ago, yes.

Vera We were kids.

Finbar We were kids – I know we were. We were
children. But I stole that fucking thing for you, yeh know.

Vera You did not!

Finbar Ooh! your people never stole anything?

Vera Did you?

Finbar Can I have another drink? (*As she pours it:*) Stole
that fuckin' pen out of Mooney's.

Vera (*extends the freedom of the bottle*) Help yourself.

Finbar Thanks. And you wrote me off.

Vera . . . No.

Finbar No?

Vera *You* were the –

Finbar No! – Vera! – Now! – You!

Vera *You* were the one who –

Finbar Oh-ho Jesus, that family of yours!

Vera There is nothing wrong with my . . . (*Automatic
defence of her family that tails off into a silent 'well'.*)

Finbar What? (*And laughs harshly at her.*)

Vera (*to herself*) Heigh-ho! (*To him:*) Yes?

Finbar They didn't like you – consorting? – with the
likes of me?

Vera Yes?

Finbar Protecting you from me?

Vera Yes?

Finbar There never was such a tale of woe than that of

Juliet and her Romeo! They were scandalised.

Vera   But you were the one who gave in to them.

Finbar   *I* was the one? – I wasn't the one!

Vera   Oh-you-were.

Finbar   Well, you can bet your sweet – Why wouldn't I be the one?!

Vera   Do you know the defiance a schoolgirl is capable of?

Finbar   . . . What?

Vera   This is childish.

She appears to dismiss the matter. But, on reflection, her stand against her family in childhood interests her. She gestures **Finbar** *to continue while she tries to work it out: perhaps she will defy her family again, with* **Finbar***: perhaps this is why she came here.* **Finbar** *laughs.*

Finbar   The pressures! Your father, Char*les* P. O'Toole, your mother, your – the fucking sheriff: they even got the superintendent of the guards in to have a word with me! Because we were *walking* out the road together! What? They brought in what-was-his-name? – Bollicky Bill – rubbing the lapels of his holy black jacket – who summoned me to the presbytery for a serious interview. If you'd had been a skivvy, a maid, he'd have made me marry you! Me, all of sixteen years of age!

Vera   They called the doctor for me to examine – my tonsils! (*And she starts laughing.*)

Finbar   They became very serious. I don't know if they considered assassination.

Vera   My mother pulled my hair –

Finbar   (*laughing harshly*)   Nickerdepazze!

Vera   The nuns sprinkled holy water – (*She demonstrates how they did it.*) – Ah-haa!

Finbar   Aw but *you* missed out on the Christian Brothers:

Wait'll I tell you –

Vera They didn't have to assassinate you. Someone got you a job: Mac – Goozelum's – messenger boy, the butcher shop. That's how they got *you*. But, a schoolgirl: I would've died for you then to go on defying them.

Finbar . . . What's up? What're you at?

Vera Nothing that I know of as yet.

Finbar Help me make it through the night.

Vera Can I stay for two nights? I'm booked to go back Wednesday morning. (*Shrugs:*) I'd prefer not to have to check in anywhere. And – twenty-four years later? – we take up where we left off. What d'you like? Anyway you like. And, bob's your uncle. D'you get *my* drift?

He nods.

Vera D'you know what I mean, Finbar?

Finbar Yeh.

Vera Settled then?

Finbar No problem.

She nods, 'settled'. They sip. Something beginning to worry him: a problem.

The car. (*She doesn't understand.*) What about your car out there? The Punjab: This is the Punjab you're in now, i.e., the New Estate!

Vera Does it matter?

Finbar As it is, there mightn't be a wheel left under it already. No, let me think this one out.

Vera Leave it until morning.

Finbar (*reflectively*) I'd better do it now while I'm drunk.

She laughs at him. Then he laughs too.

Vera Don't leave it near the hotel.

Finbar Give me the keys.

Vera Can you drive?

Finbar Ooh! Is it an aeroplane then? (*He has put on a jacket, is putting on his old overcoat:*) I'll think of some place safe. Yeh. Though I know someone will spot me: This town! (*Takes up his glass.*) What d'you think of me now is it any harm to ask?

Vera I couldn't give a fuck about you.

Finbar Here's lookin' at you, kid. (*And knocks back his drink.*) Back in a tick.

Vera We'll have a nice time.

Finbar In case you're interested: that's a candle, and my place of ablutions is out there.

He's gone.

Vera's *private self. Her gathering depression. She takes off her wig. The broken armchair, the small bed: she bows to them. She starts to undress, down to her slip. She takes something from her overnight bag, takes the candle and goes out.*

Scene Four

A long, dining-room table, antique, and some chairs: **Henry Locke-Browne**'s.

A child, seated at the table over his homework, looks lost in this space. His head comes up to think, and continues up, becoming frozen in a mystery that perhaps has no answer: **Norman**, *aged eleven.*

At a remove from **Norman**, *his back to us, standing, looking at nothing,* **Henry**.

Norman Dad?

Henry *does not register* **Norman**'s *whisper for a moment. He too is lost in this moment of time. He looks at his watch as if he were puzzled by it. He is middle-aged, a drop-out lawyer who does not* *practise; disillusioned, an alcoholic, an urbane one. The culture has defeated him. He does not know who he is. This evening – and perhaps yesterday – he is playing the role of father. His concentration span in causes/interests is short-lived. Today is his third day on the dry.*

He goes to **Norman**. **Norman** *has a problem with his homework.* **Henry** *refers him to an earlier page in a text book for the answer. He hears his wife arriving – a minor movement of his head. He refuses to be impressed by his wife.*

And **Marcia** *comes in, drawing a pushchair/pram behind her. She looks like* **Vera** *but she's bigger. Overcoat. Almost invariably her expression is one of alarm. She's not the brightest. She is trying not to make any unnecessary noise, but her face is pregnant with news. She likes to get the most out of telling a story in order to distress herself the more. She is in awe of her* **Henry**; *she loves him.*

Marcia . . . You'll never guess what.

Henry You're late.

Marcia I've good reason to be.

Henry Tck!

Marcia No, wait'll you hear.

Henry Pram?

Marcia (*silent 'oh!' then*) Sorry.

And she pushes the pushchair/pram out of the room. The pushchair/pram and its contents are not allowed in this room.

Henry (*to* **Norman** *who was interested in his mother's news*) Twenty-five minutes.

Norman *resumes working.* **Henry** *sits with a book and* **Marcia** *returns.*

Marcia . . . Vera.

Henry Yes.

Marcia (*disappointed*) Did you hear?

Henry I didn't! (*And a warning/checking glance in* **Norman**'s *direction.*)

Marcia (*distressed for a moment*) Lord!

Henry (*casually*) Is she dead?

Marcia's *superstition of his last.*
He blows a silent sigh.

Marcia She's back!

Henry Yes?

Marcia Since Monday.

Henry Yes?

Marcia Four days! – No, wait'll I tell you. And d'you know what she's doing? . . . Living with the tinkers. Henry! With that old thing, with that old sponger, that old layabout, Reilly, Finbar Reilly, the medal man, up in the New Estate.

Henry In the Punjab? (*He's interested.*)

Marcia In this town, our Vera!

Henry Norman, apply yourself!

Marcia With that old trick-o'-the-loop, that old –

Henry In the Punjab?

Marcia In the Punjab, up in the Punjab! Weren't the guards up there! Because of the car. Someone reported it – Didn't I see them myself walking round it, writing down the number!

Henry What car?

Marcia Oh, stop, Henry! The car, the car, the car sure!

Henry Hold, child. (*Then a glance at* **Norman** *to check on him.*) Twenty minutes. What car?

Marcia The big silver one! Isn't it parked in the street up the road round the corner. Four days! No one knowing whose it was or how it came to be there, someone reported it to the guards and they traced it to Dublin – Hertz! They found out it was rented to Vera in Dublin. Don't you know the way she is and sure it must've cost her the earth. How could the guards or anyone have known if she was alive or dead or kidnapped, Tom said. Tom is in a desperate state. Then someone saw Finbar Reilly skulking the back streets early the other morning and the guards drove up to him and there she was. But wait'll you hear. Because then the guards thought Tom would like to know. You know the way he worries and tries to be a father to us all.

Henry (*irritably*)   Yes-yes.

Marcia   And Tom drove up there and knocked at the door. But d'you know what she did? 'How yeh doin':' That was all he said to her! 'I only want to talk to you for a minute.'

Henry   Yes?

Marcia   She was in her underwear.

Henry   Yes?

Marcia   Slammed the door in his face. She nearly took the nose off him he said.

Henry   She was frightened of him.

Marcia (*through her tears*)   Pardon?

Henry   He frightens me.

Marcia   Tom?

Henry   Is that it?

Marcia   I thought you were going out to play bridge?

Henry   Is-that-it?!

Marcia   No. Tom and Mary Jane will be here in a minute to see Norman.

Henry   Norman?

Marcia They want to talk to Vera.

Henry What has Norman got to do with it?

Marcia (*licks her lip for the answer*) Vera has always given him money?

Henry *shakes his head.*

Marcia The Tintin comics she sends him that she reads herself?

Henry *shakes his head.*

Marcia They were writing a letter when I left them?

Henry *nods.*

Marcia It's urgent – it's very urgent – That must be them arriving now. And they were saying that if Norman took it up to her she wouldn't slam the door in *his* face. (*She is moving off.*)

Henry A moment. (*Wait a moment.*)

Marcia What is she trying to do to us?

Henry (*angrily*) Marcia!

Marcia Sorry. (*Returning obediently.*)

Henry If a child is required for this diplomatic manoeuvre why cannot one of Tom's be engaged for the purpose?

Marcia They're in Newcastle, being looked after by their granny: Caitriona's nerves are gone again.

Henry I'm not surprised.

He dismisses her and she goes out. **Henry** *has a new interest. He becomes conscious of* **Norman** *who, now, smiles at him. There is gentleness, regret in* **Henry**'s *voice:*

Twenty minutes, my son.

Mary Jane, **Marcia** *and* **Tom** *come in.*

Mary Jane *is the (smallest and) cleverest of the O'Tooles. She and*

Henry *had a romance one time: she dropped him. Something she has lost or betrayed has made her hard, cynical, impatient – and innocent. On this occasion she tries to rein herself, putting up with* **Tom**. *(She and* **Tom** *have done a deal and she does not want to lose her part of it.) Refer* **Henry***'s description of her, Scene Six.*

Tom. *Refer* **Henry***'s and* **Vera***'s remarks, Scene Six. He looks an inoffensive type. His jacket is never unbuttoned. It is difficult to insult him. (Or this is a defence mechanism, now ingrained in him, adopted from the culture.) Almost invariably he is professionally jolly or professionally sad/concerned/angry. At the moment he is sad.*

Mary Jane Oh?! *(She did not expect to find* **Henry** *in.)*

Henry *(a charming host)* Ah! Mary Jane!

Mary Jane How are you, Henry!

Henry I am very well, thank you! And you?

Mary Jane I am very well! Norman!

Tom My friend. *(His hand out for a handshake.)*

Henry *(bows, but keeps his hands behind his back)* The Irish family O'Toole! And your good husband Declan, Mary Jane?

Mary Jane He's fine! Do you have change, Tom?

Tom *(producing his wallet)* We thought we'd find you out.

Henry No, oh ho-ho, I'm in!

Tom You're a gas man.

Henry And your good wife Caitriona?

Tom But we're disturbing this man (**Norman**) in his work.

Henry Ara what! (**Henry***'s brogue: meaning 'not at all'.)*

Tom Now: For Norman. *(A fiver to* **Mary Jane**.)

Mary Jane Norman.

Norman *looks at his father.*

Henry   Accept. And give it (*to*) your mother, and she will give you a thruppence for it.

Norman   Thanks. (*And pockets the fiver.*)

Henry   I have undertaken his tutelage.

Tom   I's wonderful.

Henry   You'll take a drink: Tom, Mary Jane?

Marcia   Henry! (*Alarmed.*)

Henry (*gestures his freedom from alcohol*)   I am completing day three! I shall never again take a drink in this life: Perhaps not even in the next. Tea, woman of the house.

Tom   I can see the difference in you already.

Henry   True as Our Lady is in heaven.

Tom   Gas.

Marcia, *relieved, has gone out.* **Norman** *resumes his homework.*

Tom (*sad, sits*)   Yeh heard.

Henry   I'm sorry?

Tom *shakes his head, sadly.*

Henry (*shrugs to himself his feigned incomprehension, then brightly*)   Well, Mary Jane, you don't *look* very well!

Mary Jane   No? How are you?

Henry   Beano! Groceries selling well?

Mary Jane   Dandy!

Tom (*becomes a good sport*)   Well, ye're a nice pair the three of ye! (*He warms to himself:*) 'Twas morning last night when ye came in. Now if this's to continue it'll have to stop cause if ye want to stay here ye'll have to find somewhere else! The landlady bejakers! (*But he grows solemn again: he has produced an envelope – the letter.*) Well if this's what the world is coming to, I don't know where it's going; if this's what we're bringing up our children for: Can anyone explain that to me, Henry?

Henry   Excuse me? (*And, then, he looks at* **Mary Jane** *for an explanation or interpretation.*)

Mary Jane   Vera.

Tom   Vera.

Henry (*to himself*)   Vera?

Mary Jane   Marcia told you! (*Trace of annoyance, impatience.*)

Henry   Yes. That Vera has returned from – New York? – and something about delivering a letter – Is that the one? – and everyday, common-or-garden matters, but – Lost: what has produced this air of grief?

Tom   Did Marcia not tell you where our sister is presently residing?

Henry   Did Marcia not tell me where. . . ?

Tom   For the past four days!

Henry   I believe she – (*Thinks.*) – Yes, she did. But what is the problem?

Tom'*s mouth growing a silent, smiling 'what?'*

Mary Jane   Oh come on, Henry.

Henry   Mary Jane?

Tom   Ve-ra! Ve-ra! –

Mary Jane (*to calm him*)   Tom –

Tom   'What's the problem?'! She's us in a flaming pickle, we're in a moral fix.

Mary Jane (*to* **Tom**)   Just a sec –

Tom   Vera! When morality goes out the door anything can happen!

Mary Jane   Tom –

Henry   Not bad. (**Tom**'*s near epigram.*)

Tom   What's *your* problem, Henry?

Mary Jane   Just a sec. May I smoke?

Henry   Please.

Mary Jane   Thank you. But the point now is –

Henry   What age is she? – Excuse me, Mary Jane. Would you care to sit down? She must be forty years of age if she's a day?

Mary Jane   She's –

Tom   I don't know and I don't care what age she is but she's old enough to know better than go disgracing herself and her family and her morals in this manner. Is this what our father and mother worked hard for all their lives? What's she trying to do to us? Can she have so completely forgotten her upbringing? New York indeed and I'm sure is New York but a name means something here. It may be the nineties, (*but*) what's wrong is wrong – Even if it was the year two thousand, i's diabolical – The twenty-first century for that matter, I would be astonished and – Henry – I, for one, refuse – cannot-cannot – refuse to turn a blind eye – my conscience.

Henry   Don't follow.

Mary Jane   She's pushing thirty-eight.

Tom   All that we've been trying to do for her – for how long, Mary Jane? – Trying to look after her affairs. And now – I've a responsible government job to mind and children to rear in proper manner. And now, when her affairs are about to be finalised – and there was never any mention in the correspondence, from her or from us, about coming home, was there?

Mary Jane   No –

Tom   She arrives out of the blue and goes to live up there with your man! D'you not flaming see?

Henry   Well, when you put it that way. She must have a reason.

Tom   What?!

Henry   Yes. And, come to think of it, it is odd, strange behaviour from Vera because, I must say, I have always found her rather − shy? No?

Mary Jane   We're concerned about her, Henry.

Henry   Mary Jane? (*He's trying to bait* **Mary Jane**.) Why, I almost called her − backward. No?

Mary Jane, *refusing bait, lights her cigarette at this point.*

Henry   These affairs of hers that you've been looking after: Has anything gone awry in that department that might have upset her?

Tom   What?!

Henry   This setting up of the auction of the hotel −

Mary Jane   It's going to be a *public* auction.

Henry   Oh, I know that.

Tom   Everyone knows that!

Henry   'Deed they do, man dear alive!

Mary Jane (*to* **Tom**)   Just a second! (*To* **Henry**.)Vera isn't shy *or* backward. (*To* **Tom** *again*.) Excuse me! I think I detect something here. (*To* **Henry**.) Yes?

Henry   You're concerned about Vera, Mary Jane.

Mary Jane   We're concerned about the hotel.

Tom (*quietly*)   Yes, and −

Mary Jane (*still to* **Henry**)   We want it. Now, do you find anything odd, strange, questionable − aberrant? − in *our* behaviour!

Henry *gestures: Take the floor.*

Mary Jane   Because if you do, I'll have to say that you are frankly dafter than I thought.

Tom We're only, Henry, trying to –

Mary Jane Look! Look, we are not going to insult anybody's intelligence by explaining or discussing what is natural, reasonable, commonsensical – Excuse me, Tom! Next thing, we'd end up discussing American, hippy, gutter – mysticism! Excuse me, Tom! We want the hotel. We want to get our sister out of that place. We must. And, as it happens, we need your help. Okay so far?

Henry *gestures: She has the floor.*

Mary Jane Well, it may surprise you or it may not, Vera is a very difficult woman. I'd like to have done with this one because it's pfff-rubbish! Yes, people always commented on her shyness, even among the rest of us, the family –

Tom She wasn't like one of us at all.

Mary Jane Excuse me! Reticent nature? It's so-called. Where is she at this moment? I have always known it. Father on about her lack of 'go'. Who high-tailed it out of here – whenever she liked – Did we? Mother ranting on about her not pushing herself, taking a lead, what was to become of her. *Ranting.* Maybe that's why mother – to our surprise – left her the hotel.

Tom The woman was a saint sure –

Mary Jane Just – (*A second.*)

Tom But she wasn't right in the head towards the end.

Mary Jane For a shy person, Vera has always managed to get an extraordinary amount of attention and managed extraordinarily to do anything she liked. (*Silently:*) Oh! And the rumour – maybe you've heard it, maybe you've not – about our Vera's 'line of business' in America?

Tom What?

Mary Jane I know that Marcia hasn't heard it and I wouldn't like to be the one to mention it to her, let alone mention it in a room where there is a child.

Tom   What?

Mary Jane (*angrily*)   I told you!

Tom (*to himself; he refuses to believe the rumour*)   No.

Mary Jane (*to **Henry***)   I'm not being uncharitable.

Tom (*to himself*)   No.

Mary Jane (*continues to **Henry***)   She's not ungenerous –
oh boy can she be generous! And she's intelligent – She's
not backward: That's the maddening thing. Look! Look, I
didn't want to get into this – pfff! – at all.

Tom (*sympathetically*)   Mary Jane.

Mary Jane   I'm telling you what-we're-dealing-with: She
cannot be trusted.

Tom   She's a messer, Henry.

Mary Jane   Too many contradictions and surprises from
our Vera. And d'you know what it's all about? She thinks
she's special. Oh she *knows* that she is special. (*As if **Henry**
had contradicted her:*) But I know it! It's enough for the rest of
us to realise we have only one life to live and try to make
the best of it, Vera has to go one better. There's only one
Vera, there will never be another: not 'til or after
kingdom-come or ever. And she is being 'true' to her –
uniqueness. And while she's working out this extraordinary
individuality of hers, whatever comes into her head she's
going to do it, be it sink or swin for everyone around her.
Without thought, fear of consequences – Be it sink or swim
for *herself*! That's what we're dealing with. She's capable of
anything. Now, I don't know what her next surprise in this
present circumstance is going to be – could be a big one! –
but, if I can help it, it's not going to happen at my
expense. Or his. (**Tom**'s.)

Tom   Or Marcia's.

Mary Jane   Okay, Henry?

Henry   I could wait on your company (**Mary Jane**'s) for
ever.

Tom   Okay, Henry?

Henry   I begin to follow.

Tom (*touched*)   Do you?

Norman   Dad?

Henry (*to* **Norman**)   Five minutes.

Mary Jane   Questions?

Henry   The Imperial Hotel, this jewel in the crown of the family fortunes: (*To* **Tom**.) You will buy it at the auction.

Mary Jane   Absolutely.

Henry   Any price.

Tom   Birthright.

Mary Jane   She won't be left go short. She will get what she deserves.

Henry   I see. And the letter, Mary Jane?

Mary Jane   It's a request, simply, for her to come out and sit down with us, calmly, at a table.

Tom   Since we can't go into that 'No-Go' area.

Henry   And you want it delivered.

Mary Jane   In view of the reception she gave earlier today to Tom, his going up there again is unlikely to succeed.

Henry   Mary Jane.

Mary Jane   Marcia won't.

Henry   Yes. And?

Mary Jane   Well, I'm hardly the one to do it. I mean, to stand on some knacker's doorstep, talking to my sister in her underwear? I'd die.

Henry   Ah!

Mary Jane So, with your permission of course, Norman.

Tom Because whatever else about her you are saying, Mary Jane, she responds to children.

Mary Jane Frankly, she does.

Tom And she's always, you were saying, Mary Jane, had a special affection for Norman.

Mary Jane Who would blame her. Frankly.

Henry Check! Norman, it is time!

Tom And there are articles in the hotel that Marcia wants and should have.

Henry Now I follow.

Norman *is tidying up his books.* **Marcia** *is coming in with a tray of tea things.*

Tom The solidarity of a family in trouble.

Henry Indeed.

Tom I's moving.

Henry Oh pull back there bejesus and mind the dresser! (*Make room for* **Marcia**.) And from as far back as my young manhood I considered that family O'Toole was warmth itself. Remember, I tried not one but two of your sisters for membership. Ah, as we roved the grove summer evenings, Mary Jane's enthusiasms about daddy and mammy, Tom and her sisters, loyalties and sibling rivalries, innocent banter 'cross the table, storytelling round the hearth at night and mind the dresser there again, domesticity full of simple pleasures to scald the lonely heart of this orphan boy.

Tom Gas man.

Henry I first plied Mary Jane here with my earnest suit. Admission denied.

Tom Gas.

Henry My perseverence, bejesus, and persistence! I knocked upon Marcia's door and she took me in.

Tom Gas.

Henry You may leave.

Norman *leaves.*

Henry No, Norman.

Tom But?

Henry *smiles a 'Hmm?' to him, a 'Hmm?' to* **Mary Jane**.

Mary Jane I understand. It is always difficult for in-laws in these little family affairs. Tom, Marcia and I, somehow, the immediate family are of course the ones to deal with it.

Henry *(I)* Protest! Your attentiveness in bringing this matter to my home and including me in the family conference: Solidarity. As a first step towards resolution an interview with Finbar Reilly is crucial. Put yourselves in my hands. I shall see to it personally and at once.

Mary Jane No –

Henry Not at all! My father the colonel died in the Punjab, in a house owned by a Mrs Scarry, I believe.

Tom But – *(He has the letter in his hand.)*

Henry *(takes the letter)* That too: I shall deliver it. Brave men lived before Agamemnon, and still.

And he leaves purposefully, removing his jacket – as for a change of dress. **Marcia** *looks alarmed,* **Mary Jane** *has misgivings but it is too late,* **Tom**'s *smile is widening and beginning to freeze.*

Scene Five

Finbar's. *Candlelight. A couple of bentwood chairs and a rickety table have been called into play. (The table is 'a composite': component parts are stylistically at odds, salvaged pieces from other furniture.)*

Another light, off, in the back-kitchen — candle or flashlamp — where **Finbar** *is doing something.*

And **Vera** *is in bed, smoking, her hands behind her head, depressed. Her slip, now, is dirty and she has not brushed her hair in four days. She has decided, it appears, that as long as* **Finbar** *keeps talking she will keep singing. (The song, though no issue is made of it, was one of her grandmother's songs.)*

Vera   '. . . that's where I laboured so hard for ol' massa, day after day in the fields of yellow corn, no place on earth do I love more sincerely . . .' (*She listens.*)

Finbar (*off*)   Oh but nice clean people are the O'Tooles!

Vera   'Than ol' Virginia the land where I was born!'

Finbar *comes in with plates, bread, mugs, a tin of beans for the table. Then:*

Finbar   Wouldn't you think she'd get up!

Vera   'That's where I laboured!' –

Finbar   Wouldn't you think she'd –

Vera   'So hard for ol' massa –'

Finbar   Get dressed! –

Vera   'Day after day –'

Finbar   Wash herself! –

Vera   'In the fields of yellow corn –'

Finbar (*going out again*)   Wouldn't you think she'd! –

Vera   'No place on earth do I love more sincerely!' (*And she continues quietly:*) 'Than ol' Virginia the land where I was born.'

Finbar *is back with a tin-opener to open the tin of beans. A beat. And:*

Finbar   Two nights you asked for –

Vera   'Carry me back –'

Finbar   Two nights! you asked for for to stay here –

Vera   'To ol' Virginie, that's where the cotton –'

Finbar   Now there's four gone –

Vera   'An the corn an' taties grow –'

Finbar   Now the fifth starting! –

Vera   'That's where de birds warble sweet in the springtime –'

Finbar   Uff! (*He throws down the tin-opener – he's hurt his finger – and goes out again:*) Fuckin'!

Vera   'That's where this ol' darky's heart am long to go.' (*And she blows a sigh to herself.*)

Finbar *returns with a box of new tin-openers. He unwraps one.*

Finbar   And bringing the red-necks up here to me in their uniforms and squad car. Fuckin' guards watching every hands turn I make all my life already, and Mr Tom O'Toole after that on his BMW. Is it that you want to go bringing them up here to me again?

Vera (*to herself*)   Yeh.

Finbar   And aul' ones out there this evening, coming up here for a gawk at my house when the news had broke. Linking one another for safety: the way aul' ones like to take a look at a place where a man has hanged himself.

Vera (*reasonably*)   You fucked me twenty minutes ago.

Finbar ... (*an astonished whisper*)   What?!

Vera   He fucked me twenty minutes ago so what is he complaining about?

Finbar   Oh nice clean – Wouldn't you think she'd – And I've a man in the morning calling early about a lock of bentwood chairs! (*Completing opening the tin:*) Neglecting my business. (*And off to dump the box of tin-openers:*) Fuckin' Taiwan!

Vera (*sighs to herself*)   Oh fuck off.

Finbar (*returning*)   Nice clean people and they at one another's throats after the mother dying last year when it became known that the one in America had inherited the hotel over all their heads.

Vera (*to herself*)   Oh fuck off.

Finbar   The town is delighted. (*Then, hearing in retrospect what she said, another astonished whisper:*) What?!

Vera   Oh fuck off.

Finbar   . . . *You* fuck off!

Vera   Oh fuck off.

Finbar   *You* fuck off – *You* fuck off!

Vera   'Carry me back to ol' Virginie!'

Finbar   By Jesus, by Jesus, it's hard to credit it was from the nuns that you learned your manners!

Vera   Wouldn't you think she'd.

Finbar   What?

Vera   Wash herself.

Finbar   Wouldn't you think she would!

Vera   Look at the place! Look at the place!

Finbar   I'm looking.

Vera   How does anyone live like this?

Finbar   Ooh! –

Vera   Woodlice!

Finbar   What?

Vera   Woodlice! The place is infested with them! –

Finbar   No –

Vera   Out there – Woodlice! – waddling their lives in the dark in the damp across that floor out there! –

Finbar No! –

Vera Over there then – look at them *now*! – doing pilgrimages by candle-light up the fucking walls!

Finbar Ooh! but the O'Tooles set the highest standards –

Vera 'Carry me back! –'

Finbar Fighting like cats and dogs over property!

Vera Fuck off!

Finbar *You* fuck off, *you* fuck off, that's what *I'm* saying to *you*!

Vera How! do people live like this?

Finbar There's the door for you there!

Vera *starts whistling her song, crosses her arms – whatever: A gesture that she's staying put.*

Finbar But methinks they've come to some arrangement of late, the O'Tooles, because the tempest has died down among them. And Tom O'Toole, short of going on the radio to broadcast it, has made it known to all and sundry that he'll be bidding for the hotel at the auction. A hotel, yes, but once the family home as well and, with the clergy behind him and considering our history against the English, who will bid against an honest man attempting to get back the homestead? He'll get the place for nothing.

Vera (*blankly/blandly*) Yeh? (*But it's further news and hurt.*)

Finbar Yeh! Them are the rules. That's the way it goes.

Vera And there's a rat about the place.

Finbar A?

Vera There's a rat about the place.

Finbar No.

Vera There's a rat about, in, the place!

Finbar   No rat –

Vera   I saw him!

Finbar   No rat in –

Vera   Several times!

Finbar   No rat in this!

Vera   A rat, a fucking pet, a pet fucking rat!

Finbar   A fucking –

Vera   I feel sorry for him! – he doesn't even bother to run –

Finbar   A fucking mouse!

Vera   I don't think he's able to run!

Finbar   Keep your voice down –

Vera   He's lost heart! – who would blame him?

Finbar   Oh but they're –

Vera   Only waiting for someone to bring the back of a shovel down on his head!

Finbar   Oh but they're getting the one from America, no half measures.

Vera   How – WHY – do people live like this?

Finbar   Rooking her, screwing her – They are!

Vera (*swings her legs out of the bed*)   Heigh-fucking-why-ho!

Finbar   They are!

Vera (*slips on her shoes*)   And if you move anything: tawny, yellow, almost see-through, fast-moving strings of evil-looking fucking things that move in and out precisely.

Finbar   They are!

Vera   And this poxy little bed that would cripple you. (*She stands.*)

He watches her suspiciously. (He's frightened of her.) She gets her handbag without knowing what she wants from it. She produces an aerosol tin of something from it and throws it aside onto the floor. She turns her bag upside down, spilling the contents onto the bed and she stares with puzzlement down at them.

Finbar (*through the above*) They are! ... So they are ... I don't know yet where the in-laws fit in.

Vera Cockroaches in New York?

Finbar But I'm working on it.

Vera All this place needs is seagulls. (*She takes a mug from the table and she goes out.*)

Finbar (*calls after her*) His majesty, Mr Henry Locke-Browne, Lord Henry, barrister-at-law who doesn't practise and friend of the working classes! (*He picks up the aerosol tin, returns it to the contents of her bag. To himself:*) No rat in this. (*Calls:*) Or 'The doctor's daughter', Caitriona, Mr Tom O'Toole's missus, Caitriona! (*The contents of her bag are on the bed in front of him. He steals some money out of her wallet:*) But I'm working on it. So I am. But I'm the one in all this is going to end up in handcuffs. (*Calls:*) Or the other fella, Mary Jane's fella, Mr Declan Mansfield, the wanker with the supermarket and the straight white eyelashes!

Vera *returns, sipping water from the mug. A quietness, a 'politeness', about her, a new mood. (Perhaps she smiles – winks broadly – at him, which frightens him even more.) She sits on the bed, raking a finger through the contents of her bag. A feel, just a touch, to her wallet.*

Finbar Because it's my business to know the O'Tooles' business and everybody else's business in this town. And that's for sure.

Vera Today is Thursday, yeh? (*She has taken up an airline ticket.*)

Finbar All day.

Vera (*reading airline ticket*) Dublin–New York, 'Okay, Okay.' This was for yesterday morning. Okay. (*And she tears it up.*)

So that one's okay.

Finbar (*indicates the table*)   If she wants something to eat.

Vera (*absently*)   Hmm?

Finbar   Oh well, if she doesn't want it. (*The food.*)

Vera   No thanks. (*Like talking to herself:*) You're making statements about my family: I want you to stop. Okay? Okay. They mean an awful lot to me. So they do. They keep me going. Life-long fear that I might be on my own. Out there in space like a fucking astronaut with his tube cut. Did you see that one? (*She's probably talking about a film.*) Life-long fear of just going to sleep, afraid to let go. So they've been a great help. (*A second airline ticket, looking at it:*) Thursday, you say, Finbar. This one's for tomorrow. New York–Atlanta, 'Okay, Okay.' Some hope Atlanta now. (*Tears up second ticket:*) So that one's okay too. So what am I do? Because I was meant to be in Atlanta, Georgia, tomorrow to entertain some cavalry. A weekend-long affair. It was on the strength of that (*job*) that I came home. I got an advance from the man because the man likes me. Still, the man would throw you out a window or in the river if a cavalry party he set up went short of meat. 'Specially paid-for meat. Maybe I would do the same to him or better. Caviare and a little mercury. So I want you to stop making statements about my family because now I've got problems both sides of the Atlantic. (*She has an impulse to laugh.*) Okay?

Finbar   What did *I* say?

Vera   My family keep me going. I've been in situations you cannot even imagine. That *I* cannot even imagine. Up there, down there. (*Highs and lows.*) Did anyone ever tell you to eat shit? Human excrement, shit. No? But I survived – up there, down there – came out on top of! – situations because of – y'know? So I want you to stop. Okay ... See these? (*A small container of pills.*) My Xanadus I call them. These can ease things. Human excrement, shit, shits, become more palatable with these. Working girls, friends of mine, use them on themselves. I don't much use them on myself. I prefer to use them more for the purpose of taming a difficult client, anaesthetising an animal. And not for all the fucking tea in China, the coffee in Brazil would I take one of them now.

Finbar If I hurt your feelings.

Vera (*rises*) One of these'd put manners on a mustang. (*She puts them on the table:*) So I keep these in reserve. I could tell you things if I wanted to.

Finbar I said I'm sorry if I –

Vera How to kill someone? (*Turns on him.*) Caviare and a little mercury? I learned more at school from the nuns than loving chastity above all things. D'you read me? – God bless yeh! – D'you get my drift?

Finbar Don't come near me – !

Vera Who d'you think you're dealing with?

Finbar Stay where –

Vera Who is the whore?

Finbar I never called you a –

Vera Who is the whore? –

Finbar I don't know what you're talking about! –

Vera Okay? Okay? –

Finbar Stop! – Fuckin'! – Jesus! –

He is retreating, she keeps following. Though her attack on him is blind it is slow-moving – at least it is at first. She follows with her face thrust out. Now she is swinging her hands at him:

Vera Okay? Okay? . . .

Finbar Fuckin'! Jesus! Stop!

Vera *hits him a few clatters. She is going to hit him again:*

Finbar (*hits her. Then*) You cunt! (*A beat, and he hits her again.*) You cunt! . . . (*Frightened:*) I told you! . . . That's what you get . . . I warned you.

She is hurt – holding her head and doubled over. But now she starts laughing – terrible laughter – and now she is pursuing him again, for more, laughing, her face thrust out. He gets out of the room, to the front of the house, to the hall. She behaves as if he had never been in the room.

Vera Okay? . . . Fuck me, screw me, rook me – if-you-are-able! – but don't anyone of you insult me like this! Okay? . . . I'm someone, amn't I? . . . Who-what *am* I? A hole between my legs? . . . I'm not a cunt . . . (*I'm*) Someone. Okay, (*I'm*) someone on my own then – I'm not going to be afraid of that. Life-long fucking fear of – are you kiddin'?! Okay . . . *Who* is the whore? – Quem, cunt, ghee, box, slash, gash, cock-sucking, grandmother-fucking piece of shit, daff, crap, excrement? *Me*?! . . . (*Asking herself:*) Look, what do you want? Tell me. This? (**Finbar**'s *place.*) Revenge: is that what you want? The hotel? More hotel-fucking-rooms? Fucking family? (*She doesn't know. She sits.*) All dirt and lies. Well, look at it: Dirt. Lies. All fucked. All over. There: buy a child for a dollar, cheaper than a chicken; here: go fuck your grandmother . . . (*She becomes conscious of becoming tearful and of being alone; then, in reaction, baby voice:*) Aaw, have they gone and left you on your own? Is Baby Vera lonely-wonely? A-a-a-w! (*Followed by several mock sob-sniffles, derisive of herself. Then:*) Don't be so fucking stupid. Get up! (*Rises. Shouts after* **Finbar**:) You! If you'd stop, let me think what I should do, I would fuck off and do it! Okay? (*Sits again. I'm.*) Fucking crazy, nuts. But one of these days, Baby Vera, you're going to have to pull that tiny mind of yours together. (*She realises that she is seated again:*) What?! Get up! (*Starts to rise, does not manage it the first time; then:*) Get up, cunt! (*And stands defiantly, legs apart:*) See! Okay? Okay . . . (*She sees* **Finbar** *returning:*) You! –

Finbar (*is alarmed and pacificatory*)   No, I swear – solemn oath – I'm not – There's someone coming in the!

Vera *starts laughing at him. She takes up a mug or a plate or plates.*

Finbar No, Vera – Please – at the gate – Maybe the guards again –

Vera The money you stole from my wallet!

Finbar Aw Jesus, I would never –

Vera Twice!

Finbar No, Vera – Don't!

She has gone out with mug/plates and fires them. They smash outside.

Vera Fuck off! (*And she is returning for further missiles.*)

Finbar Fuckin' Jesus –

Henry (*off*) Don't shoot!

Finbar Please – Fuckin' – Stop!

Henry (*off*) Don't shoot! Don't shoot! Friend! A friend!

Henry *is outside. He has drink taken but he can carry it. He is wearing an old-fashioned coat (a type of black frock-coat), carries a cane and a black hat. (He produces the letter later.)*

Finbar Who? (*To himself.*)

Henry Finbar? Finbar? Henry Locke-Browne!

Finbar Henry Locke-Browne. He has the suit on.

Henry I have come unarmed and alone! Don't shoot! I come as a messenger!

Finbar I'll have to go out to him. Will I?

Henry Let down the bridge! I pray you in the name of the Most High!

Vera *goes out to* **Henry**, *as for a confrontation, but his style – unorthodox attire and greeting – appeal to her, privately.*

Vera Yeh!?

Henry Good Lord! I'd no idea you were such a handsome woman!

Vera   Yeh!?

Henry   May I come in?

She returns to the room. He follows.

How are you, Finbar!

Finbar   I'm not so bad at all, Henry, how's yourself!

Henry   Plu-perfect! For you. (*Gives the letter to* **Vera**.) It's from your brother Tom and sister Mary Jane.

Vera   And your wife?

Henry   No. At very best, Marcia's a bit-player in the plot: She's been promised the trinkets. I shouldn't bother to read it: It's a horrible composition. I steamed it. I'd ask you to put your shoes on and come out for a drink but the authorities are uncommonly active this evening about the licensing hours. Something has upset them. The sergeant himself is posted on the usually dependable Mannions of the Hollow.

Finbar   They're after promotion all right.

Henry   You don't have something in the house by any chance?

There is nothing to drink in the house.

Finbar   They become very dedicated when they're upset.

Vera (*tears the letter in two*)   Fuck this for a game of toy soldiers. I know where there's plenty of drink. Would you like a drink?

Henry   I could be persuaded.

Vera   Would you like a drink?

Finbar   I don't mind. But I've a man in the morning calling early about a lock of bentwood chairs.

During the above, **Vera** *dressing – simply, her mac over her slip – while* **Finbar** *is finding his old overcoat. She puts the pills she left on the table into her pocket, collects her bag and leads them off.*

Scene Six

Street-light coming up and in, colouring rather than lighting the dark; vague shapes that will turn out to be a piano, an upholstered couch and armchairs draped in dust-sheets: an upstairs room in the hotel, overlooking the square.

Off, below, a glass shattering. (A window.)

And, after a few moments, **Vera**, **Henry** *and* **Finbar** *come in.* **Vera** *has her overnight bag. (***Vera***'s silence.)*

Henry   Up here you would have us?

Finbar   I was in the back bar down there all right a couple of times . . .

Henry (*moves to the window to look down at the square, left and right*)   No. No.

Finbar   But I was never up here.

Henry   Not a soul. The enemy sleeps.

Finbar   I cut my hand.

Henry   This is georgian!

Finbar   Is it, it's not.

Henry   Originally, actually, Queen Anne. Though, if we could see, you'd hardly credit it now.

Finbar   You're not serious! (*He isn't interested, and he is talking in whispers.*)

Henry   Mm! Seventeen-o-seven, I think it was, the site was acquired for to build a dower-house for one Maria Locke, a distant cousin of my own on my mother's side. (*He finds a switch and tries it:*) It don't work, Inspector. (*And tries another.*)

Finbar (*sniggers*)   Maybe someone didn't pay the bill.

Henry   I know I've seen Tom and Mary Jane go in and out of here at night, I know I've seen a light. And Marcia.

Finbar   The mainswitch.

Henry   Where is the mainswitch? . . . Vera?

Vera   Oh. Downstairs. There's a storeroom off the kitchen we came through.

Henry   You understand such matters, Finbar.

Finbar   A switch? A child would! . . . A switch whether it's main or not is only a switch. (*But he goes out:*) I'm not a maid.

Henry   . . . Poor dumb building: The innocence of it.

Silence.

I should go perhaps and assist him? (*A movement to leave perhaps.*)

Vera   This is where I was born.

Henry   I'm sorry?

Vera   What do I do with it? . . . Why didn't they ask me for it?

Henry   Ask?

Vera   Yeh. Rigmaroles about auctions.

Henry   You are not an innocent.

Vera   No. I have my problems but I'm not an innocent. But that's all they had to do. I think.

Henry   Are you really not one of us?

Vera   What? (*Her head turns to him, perhaps for the first time.*)

Henry   To ask for something, surely, would sound suspiciously uncomplicated.

Vera   Why did my mother leave it to me?

Henry   To take a last harsh laugh to the grave?

She laughs with her breath in the dark – incidentally, a sound rather like crying.

. . . You are cross with them.

Vera They're so – busy. And do they get any special comfort from it, do they? . . . I'm cross with myself. All my life the feeling of belonging has eluded me: Why should I go on thinking I'll find it? The thought of here *hasn't* kept me going: the thought of here cripples me . . . (*To herself:*) Yeh know?

Henry Yeh. (*To himself.*)

Vera . . . Why is Mary Jane supporting Tom?

Henry Greed. It is the only passionate sensation that moves her. She will die of it. She has taken poison and become some sort of nervous stick with a criminal's mind. She should be locked up. Anything that does not add to her life will be substracted from it. Mary Jane: And what she once was. (*He reins himself in the next:*) Why, she has castrated that poor shopkeeping husband of hers . . . and . . .

Vera She despises him for allowing her to do it.

Henry *She* is the innocent. But I've been mixing some metaphors – I am fond of a mixed metaphor – And I speak out of turn?

Vera No; I'm getting used to it. And my brother believes, he *really* believes everything he himself says.

Henry It gives him a headache.

Vera Why are they doing this together?

Henry Team spirit. Are you really not one of them? It is a clanship between night-runners, a collaboration. And one, I am sure, containing the usual, concessional understanding: That, whereas, when he tumbles the sheep she will get the hindquarters . . . I should not take it too personally to heart. These marauding family expeditions happen on a national scale. A member of course is sacrificed, but it is done for the greater good of the pack.

Vera What's in it for you?

Henry Rescue me ... I jest. I should like to exceed the deeds of my father. (*You are a very handsome woman.*)

Vera What is it worth?

Henry Two-eighty thousand? Thereabouts ... It doesn't bring a smile to your face?

Vera What do I do with it?

Henry Sell it ... You don't want money?

Vera I want-need-money but –

Henry Put yourself in my hands – no fees. Withdraw it from auction – You are not bound to the auction – put a price on it and sell by private treaty. To Tom if you wish –

Vera I don't know that I –

Henry Dick or Harry then. That's what your brother's emotion will do with it if he gets it: He'll sell it. He'll first get large grants off the Tourist Board to do it up, then – The silk of my degrees is at your disposal.

Vera I don't know that I want to sell to anyone.

Henry Lease it. For an income ... Keep it.

Vera I don't want it. No: This, I think, is going to be my last throw in the game of family and, if that is so, I want to do something more than selling, keeping, leasing.

Henry Those are the options.

Vera Burn it to the ground?

Henry ... By Jesus yes! The generosity of it! Now I follow! Put it to the torch, leave it in ashes and I'll purify myself in the flames with you bejesus! And we'll hike it out of here the two of us together – without baggage! – for a land I will show you where they do not make you sick discussing the cherished values that are under threat and their duties to the great God they've reduced to a huckster.

A light comes on on the landing, a spill from it coming into the room.

Quick, your instructions!

Finbar (*off*)   They're on!

Vera (*switches on a light*)   I want to see them.

Henry   Do not underestimate them.

Vera   We wait. Let *them* make the next move.

Finbar (*coming in*)   They're on.

Henry   Bejesus they are, they're on!

Vera (*to* **Finbar**)   Thanks –

Henry   I'll draw the drapes.

Vera   No.

Henry   No drapes?

Vera   Why? (*She switches on another light.*)

Henry   I like it.

Finbar   What? (*He does not know what is going on.*)

Vera   What are these? (*Rolls of architect's drawings she has picked up off a chair.*)

Henry   What did I tell you! Architect's drawings. Someone – already! – has plans for your property. Yes, our affairs are critical but first things first: What're we all having?

Vera (*dumps the drawings*)   What would you like?

Henry   What would you like, Finbar?

Finbar   What're you having yourself, Vera?

Vera   Champagne?

Finbar   Champagne? Hydrogen!

Henry (*sharply*)   A pint is out of the question.

Finbar (*just as sharply*)   I know that, I'm not a fool.

Henry   Any kind of whiskey.

Finbar   Same.

Vera   With?

Henry   Half-and-half.

Finbar (*nods. And*)   If you please.

Vera   Okay.

She leaves.

Finbar *frowning 'What?', and frowning suspiciously, watching* **Henry** *during the following.*

And **Henry** *sets to work, putting away his hat and cane, removing dust-sheets, folding them, arranging furniture to his taste, busy concentration, talking to himself. (The piano is left covered.)*

Henry   Yes I like her, yes I do – (*Winks at* **Finbar**:) We're on a good thing. To work, Henry: put away your cap and cane, we might as well be making a start. Yes I do. And she has the stuff bejesus to immortalise herself in this town, and maybe rescue you as well. Why, she is a veritable Achilles if you want my opinion – and Mary Jane's, oh-ho-ho! No buying or selling or leasing for Achilles. There was only one of him and there'd never be another and he knew it. He was the man to take the head off a daisy.

Finbar   What?

Henry   By Jesus the skin and hair is going to fly at last.

Finbar   What?

Henry   And her deportment is remarkable – Yes I grow inordinately fond of her. And she is still in her fitness and flowering, more or less.

Finbar   What?

Henry   What more is there to say? And will she do the *other* thing? Oh-ho-ho! And what is more, she will do it without emotional imposition! Think of that.

Finbar   What?

Henry   Or inhibition.

Finbar   What?

Henry   Heroically. Yes, let them off and welcome – if that's what keeps them happy: Their ceremonials and rituals, play-acting superstitions – Stolen from the Jews bejesus! – if that's what they think is the purpose of existence.

Finbar   Shouldn't the curtains be –

Henry   What? But we know better. Yes, because the purpose, the true essence and the core of all things is the ecstasy in the act of copulation. No, there is nothing like a bit of jack.

Finbar (*frustrated; indicating the lights and the window*)   Like a fuckin' lighthouse!

Henry   How are we doing, Henry? Your assistance! (**Finbar**'s.) We're nearly there.

Finbar *assists* **Henry**, *folding the largest dust-sheet.*

Henry   So, we must be brave. Unless they get her first of course. What? No. What? . . . (*Briefest glance towards the window.*) No, curtains-drapes shall not prevail against us: Out in the open, I like it. Why, man dear alive, once on a high and windy hill, a maiden, her blue knickers down around her ankles and the wind whistling through the hairs of my balls.

Finbar   Fuckin'!

Henry   And the world stood still.

Finbar (*whispering*)   Shh, she's back! (*To* **Vera**.) You're back!

Vera *entering with a tray of glasses, water, whiskey.*

Henry   Shh she's back and she wasn't too long about it at all now! Now! isn't this nice: Neat? Tidy? (*His preparation of the room.*)

Vera   Sit.

They sit. She pours the drinks.

Henry   . . . My word is my bond, true as Our Lady is in Heaven, and to be pragmatic as the politician said to the Nation.

Vera (*giving* **Finbar** *his drink*)   Hmm?

Finbar   Thank you.

Vera (*giving* **Henry** *his drink*)   Hmm?

Henry   We wait for them.

Finbar   What?

Henry   Good health!

Finbar   Good!

Vera (*raises her glass*)   And, meanwhile, there's plenty more where this came from. (*She goes to the window – as to watch and wait.*)

Silence. They sip.

Finbar   What?

And, the lights fading, **Henry***, content, starts to sing quietly to himself:*

Henry   'Breeng (*Bring*) flowers of the rarest, breeng blossoms of the fairest, from garden and hillside and woodland and dell; our hearts are full swelling, their glad voices telling, the praise of the loveliest flower of the May: O Mary we crown thee with . . .'

Interval.

The lights come up and it is now near dawn. And dawn will move into morning.

The strangely attired party continues: **Vera***'s mackintosh hanging open over her slip. Her black eye.* **Finbar***, throughout, in his old raincoat;* **Henry** *in his frock-coat.*

The bottle/s and the water jug are on the floor and they lean forward out of their seats for them as required. (There is no table.) They are now animated in their individual ways and, generally, they find even their most ordinary remarks hugely entertaining. Something perverse/ anarchic in how they complement one another with laughter.

Vera   This room, this room, this very room – !

Finbar   Vera – (*Meaning: Yes, he's listening.*)

Vera   The day my father was buried –

Henry (*gesturing at the ceiling*)   Good Lord, Queen Anne! –

Vera   I don't know where the table is gone to –

Finbar (*to* **Henry**)   Let Vera – (*Let her speak.*)

Vera   But after the funeral, that day, my mother gathered us all here and the table was there and my father's things were laid out on it – you know, the things he kept about him –

Finbar   Personal effects! –

Vera   For each of us, myself, Tom, Marcia and Mary Jane, to pick something –

Henry   Vera –

Vera   I was called first – I was *honoured*! –

Finbar   You were –

Vera   But mother was both testing me and trying to train me –

Finbar   Aw she wouldn't do –

Vera   Judging me! Well, us all! But, for instance, his wallet was there, which she said was 'intact' – (*Laughter.*)

Finbar   Did *you* get that?

Vera   Mary Jane.

Henry   Ah!

Vera   Then Tom selected a sort-of small white pin,

symbol of something – I think he still wears it sometimes in his lapel –

Finbar   The White Star! (*To* **Henry**:) Remember them? – The symbol of a clean tongue.

Henry   'Flaming'! –

Finbar   Fuckin'!

Henry   Every time I meet your brother I think of Joan of Arc: Flaming.

Vera   But Tom wanted something else –

Henry   The last argument of the Church will always be the stake –

Finbar   Let Vera, Henry –

Vera   He didn't stand back from the table: (*He*) Looked at my mother like this – (*She demonstrates.*) – And my mother – (*Demonstrates her mother's expression and nod to* **Tom**.) And he took the watch – (*Laughter.*) – And you won't like this: But Marcia – (*She is laughing:*) Marcia's turn and, first, she took the pioneer pin – my father never drank –

Laughter. **Henry** *raises an elegant glass –*

Vera   Then she took collar-studs, a coloured handkerchief, the rosary beads, two fountain pens and a packet of Rennies! You know those things for –

Finbar   Indigestion! Ah no! –

Vera   Yes! – (*Laughter.*) –

Finbar   What did you get, Vera?

Vera   I got his, I took his – (*Trying to control her laughter:*) My father's pipe! – (*Laughing: A genuine question:*) Am I a fool?

Finbar   That's a nice memory.

Vera   Is it?

Henry   (*I*)   Hate Catholics.

Finbar You're a Catholic!

Henry Ah! But Protestant and protesting genes: my mother's side, the Lockes. By Jesus, (*there*) wasn't a member of that family – man or woman – couldn't tumble down the finest staircase without injury to limb or loss of a drop to their glasses! (*Laughter.*) –

Finbar (*to* **Vera**) D'you know what a thurible is? –

Henry That's where I get it from.

Finbar A thurible –

Henry (*to the ceiling*) Good Lord, Queen Anne: Out of what was elegance they have made a pig's mickey! (*Laughter.*) –

Vera A thurible, Finbar.

Finbar Thing for burning incense that you swing? Well, that school I was in in Connemara –

Henry Letterfrack, the borstal?

Finbar (*touchy*) Letterfrack, Connemara. Borstal, Industrial School – all right? Establishment.

Vera Finbar. (*She's listening.*)

Finbar There's a graveyard there with one hundred children.

Henry Thurible!

Finbar You're fuckin'! (*Distracting me.*) But there was a coonic back there in the area anyway, a priest (*who*) used to come in to say Mass. Thurible: I'm holding it: two or three – like lozengers (*lozenges*) – burning, glowing, in the bowl. The coonic then: little silver spoons of incense in on top of the lozengers. But I'm in charge, swinging it, keeping it going for your man while he's, yeh know, *Dominus vobiscum*, his other business, until he needed it. This was on the altar. But I mustn't have been minding my business anyway, 'cause didn't I set him on fire. What? Aw Jesus! – Smoke! – His vestments! The fuckin' coonic caught fire!

(*Laughter*.) – Oh but in the sacristy afterwards: 'I'm sorry, Father, I'm sorry!' – (**Finbar**'s *hands covering his head: The beating he received*.) – Fuckin'! Did he give me the! (*Beating*.) 'I'm sorry, Father, I'm sorry!' (*Laughter*.)

Vera   I used to watch my father. I never saw him angry.

Henry   You didn't!

Vera   I never saw him the other way either: You know? The idea of gaiety made him – (*She does it: 'Close his lips'*.) –

Finbar   'I'm sorry, Father, I'm. . . !' –

Henry   My father, the colonel: Developed taste for Bushmills whiskey and young women – women all-sorts. Died in – parlour? – of a neighbour of yours, Finbar. But you knew that of course?

Finbar *manages to nod yes and no* –

Henry   Mama misinterpreted. Why wouldn't she, the creature? Sitting at home alone, contemplating, I am sure, the social masquerade about her. (*The*) Meaninglessness of – it all! Protestant friends fled – Forty – Sixty thousand of them in our own lifetime?! – father out riding, myself at boarding-school. How was she in her own country – her own home! – to survive her – homelessness! And she comes up with the notion – Suggests desperation. Worse: Long-distance suicide? The aberrant notion of escaping it here by going off to Kenya of all places to become some kind of lay, Protestant missionary *nun*, God love her. And died there – Kenya! – the creature, before she could lift a blessed finger to relieve the lot of our black brethren – (*Laughter*.) The colonel then, to be sure, renewed vigour, up on his horse – his steed – up to your place, Finbar –

Finbar   Aw he was some – (*Man*.)

Henry   Like an ageing Ulysses bejesus, up to the Punjab, Nighttown, for a breath of fresh air! (*Laughter*.) The outcome was predestined – of course it was: He would be beaten. But, by going out, offering defiance – grinning yellow lecherous teeth back at what *they* had on offer – he

would not be *completely* beaten – (*Laughter.*) – But d'you see
what I mean!

Finbar   Some man all right the colonel – No but, Vera,
you're given a hundred pounds by your –

Henry   *O mio babbino caro!*

Finbar   No but, Vera –

Henry   A man of mighty thews! Sorry, Finbar: I
interrupted you. *Your* family.

Finbar   Ah, I'm grand.

Henry   Who was your father?

Finbar   . . . Maybe he was the same man as yours.

Henry   Maybe he?

Vera *is laughing and, because she is, though he has taken offence at
the above,* **Finbar** *starts to laugh too.*

Henry   Common father to us both: quite possible – and
acceptable: But where does it leave the virtue of *one* of the
mothers? – (*Laughter.*)

Vera (*now becoming sentimental – maudlin? – throws her arms
around* **Henry**)   I've always wanted – all my life! – to
celebrate something in this town: To do something – you
know? – without being judged – without caring whether I
was judged or not – D'you know what I mean?

Henry ⎫   Yes –

Finbar ⎭   Yes – But you're given –

Vera   Without the advice or consent of anyone, for God's
sake!

Finbar   But you're given –

Vera   I ask you! Not that I ever wished anyone or
anything dead here, but I used to think that when they did
– Lord be good to them! – so what? It's no longer going

to matter to them or embarrass them! – I'd have one
right crazy rave-up of a party.

Henry (*a toast*) A woman of necessity, a boy for pleasure,
a goat for ecstasy!

Finbar That's a *disgusting* – (*thing to say. But the others are
laughing and he laughs too.*) No but, you're given – You're
given, Vera, you're given a hundred pounds by your wife
to go to the fair and you have to come home with a
hundred animals. Now, the animals cost five pence each for
a sheep, a pound for a cow and a fiver for a horse –

Henry What is this?

Finbar No! Vera. Now, you have to buy some of each
and they must add up to, add up to a hundred, and –
And! – you can't bring home change out of the hundred
pounds –

Henry What is he talking about?

Finbar No! How many of each kind of animal d'you
come home with?

Henry (*to himself*) What!

Finbar Vera.

Vera I don't know.

Finbar . . . You do.

Vera I don't! –

Finbar You do –

Vera I'm no good at sums.

Finbar I'll give you a clue.

Henry What *is* this?

Finbar Work for a start – Work for a start, Vera, in
multiples of twenty.

Henry What?! Stop this! This is oral sex, Irish style, you
are engaging in.

Finbar That's a *dis*! (*Disgusting thing to say.*)

But **Vera** *and* **Henry** *are laughing.*

Vera My Uncle Stephen!

Henry Mm, Stephen! –

Finbar The Odeon! –

Vera The Odeon Cinema, The Wool Stores, the other things he owned. Well, he was an A-okay all right-guy – yeh? – I think. But, my father had died rather suddenly, and he nearly died without making a will, and, so, now, my mother started to work on Uncle Stephen – I'm sure of it! Reminding him that he was three years older than my father, that he was living alone – And he was a bachelor.

Finbar I've a better one than that –

Henry Finbar! (*Listen.*) –

Vera Anyway, she frightened him, and on the fear of sudden death Uncle Stephen came to live with us here –

Henry Vera –

Vera And this room again! – Shortly afterwards – I don't know where the table's got to – my mother assembled us all here again, this time around our Uncle Stephen. I mean the man was sitting there! Tom got his house – I mean, the man was sitting there – *alive!* Mary Jane got the Odeon and the little shop next door to it –

Finbar The Magnet.

Vera Marcia?

Henry Shamrock Ballroom – White elephant.

Vera Shamrock. Anyway, my mother took my shoulder to pull me forward to the table – like this. Because The Wool Stores had been earmarked by her for me. Tom – he was only a youngster! – nodding, encouraging me. My mother – (*Pulling her forward to the table.*) – Like as if the Wool Stores were on top of the table! The man was upset!

I didn't take them.

Finbar No!

Vera (*a bit lost – though laughing*) What am I talking about? I mean, *should* I have taken them? *Am* I a fool? All my life? What's my point?

Henry (*going out with empty jug*) The danger to one's immortal soul of dying intestate.

Laughter. (Though **Finbar** *is now growing self-conscious, and he would like to apologise for hitting her earlier.)*

Vera (*half to herself*) Tom got The Wool Stores too. Wait a minute! There was an agreement – a *deal* – between my mother and Tom – maybe between her and the others as well – that when he started working he would pay *her* for getting Uncle Stephen's property and because he – maybe the others too – never came across with the money, she left this place to me. Is that my point? I have to get out of these. (*Clothes. Instead, she tops up her drink.*)

Finbar (*nods at the window*) The dawn.

Vera Yes. Good. You're not going to fall asleep on me?

Finbar ('*No.*') I'm sorry for hitting you.

Vera It was honest.

Finbar What?

Vera It was honest, Finbar. D'you know what I mean, Finbar? Isn't that life?

Finbar (*is moved, grateful to her. Something nice to tell her*) D'you know anything about pyramids?

Henry (*returning with a jug of water*) Well, ye're a nice pair the three of ye!

Finbar How d'you keep a razor blade sharp? Vera.

Henry How d'you keep a razor blade sharp? Finbar.

Finbar A pyramid!

Henry Come again?

Finbar We're not fools, Henry!

Henry Never said –

Finbar I'm not talking a big fuckin' Egyptian thing! I shouldn't have. (*He regrets using offensive language about pyramids.*) I'm talking a small one, to scale – I've one at home I made myself: a model. It's only six inches high but if you put a razor blade into it – that's why I made it! – but with the cutting edges facing east and west, it keeps sharp. I don't know how many shaves I can get out of a blade.

Vera I heard about them.

Finbar Yes!

Vera People meditate in them.

Finbar If you make one big enough, to sit in. It depends on what you want to do with your pyramid. Or milk for instance will keep in them. They work.

Vera How?

Finbar Ions.

Henry What else!

Finbar No, Henry! – There's more. Dimensions – Energy: The 'just' dimensions, 'divine' proportions!

Vera What did you make your one out of?

Finbar Cardboard. The Rishis and the Devas of the Third Root Race handed down the knowledge to teachers, initiates, Vera. Modern skills, going to the moon? Child's play to them. They'd have gone there if they wanted to. They were Priest-Architects. And it was all here – not up there, the moon, *or* heaven. Here on earth. I know I'm only talking Mickey-fuckin'-Mouse about razor blades and milk. They knew *real* wonders, *real* wonders *they* worked. People out there are impressed because the tractor took over from the fuckin' horse. But the *real* knowledge is lost.

Not just calculations – Wisdom! And I think it's lost
because the teachers, who could have become initiates,
became violent.

Henry (*impressed by* **Finbar**'*s sincerity*) Mmmm!

Finbar (*grows self-conscious and laughs*) Nickerdepazze!

Henry Nickerdepazze!

Vera (*she could be talking to herself*) Being fostered out was
not an unusual thing in the past. But the reason why I was
sent to live with my grandmother was – has-to-be: She had
a farm. They wanted her to sign it over. Because there
were rows: 'I'm not dead yet' sort of rows that I didn't
understand then. And because my beloved grandmother
wouldn't sign the farm over to them, to punish her they
brought me home. Yeh, I think that's my point. (*Gets up,
collects her overnight bag:*) Let's see what I've got in here. Or
maybe there's something of my mother's (*Clothes. She goes to
the window:*) People are going up to Mass.

Henry The pious shuffle is precise, the piety is exact.

Vera (*an imperitive*) Don't go to sleep on me, *either* of you!
(*She goes out with her bag.*)

Finbar (*stands, whispers*) What?

Henry Yes I like her, yes I do, and if she has a single
flaw other than that her shoulders are a fraction high, a
trifle square, I cannot see it – One for the road for you,
Finbar – what more is there to say? (*He has gone into action:
The remains of a bottle into* **Finbar**'*s glass. He wants to get rid of*
Finbar.) Now, knock this back you.

Finbar (*whispers*) Where's she gone to?

Henry Why are the Chinese slant-eyed? – Because when
they come down in the morning they say O Jesus not rice
again. No don't sit down again – Your bentwood chairs.

Finbar What about them?

Henry You've a man calling early about a lock of bentwood chairs.

Finbar (*dismisses the chairs*) I'll tell *you* one –

Henry I've business to discuss with her. On my oath: Family matters – I've become her legal representative.

Finbar You're drunk.

Henry I'm?

Finbar We've been up all night: it's gone eight o'clock in the morning!

Henry I'm! (*He's proud of his drinking prowess.*)

Finbar (*sits?*) I'm not a married man.

Henry I'm sorry? You're not a married – What're you talking about?

Finbar Nothing! You tell *me* what I'm talking about.

Henry 'He's not a married man.'

Finbar Oh yes, it's all right for the likes of you to talk to me but it's a different matter for the likes of me to say anything to you.

Henry Haven't the foggiest idea what you are –

Finbar Sex.

Henry True as Our –

Finbar She's your fuckin' sister-in-law! Sex! Amn't I watching the two of you all night? And fuckin' incest! Don't-tell-me! Fathers and their daughters – Fuckin' clergy! Driving round the country, screwing young ones in their Volkswagens, then going home (*and*) doing their housekeepers – Sex! Christian Brothers in the schools – (*Intensely, to himself:*) Faaack! Beating the children, Henry, then buggering them: I was 'in care', Henry, them establishments, Henry? (*Pulls himself back somewhat:*) And young ones and aul' ones getting pregnant and praying to fuckin' statues about it. Country is rotten with it. (*He finds*

himself in the window.) But what else was the country taught
to think about?

Henry   There's worse! (*Coming to the window.*)

Finbar   I wish I was a bigger man.

Henry   Respectability!

Finbar   Don't tell me anything.

Henry   Their use of it.

Finbar   They're looking up at us – (*Retreating from window.*)

Henry   Respectability: the miserable tragedy. It can
absorb anything – it is unbeatable – you cannot even insult
it! (*He laughs, probably at himself.*) And I betrayed my genius
to become part of it!

Finbar (*intensity of hatred; and, as well as everything else, he
resents* **Henry**'s *ability to continue in the window*)   Fuck you.
And the colonel and mama. And Herr the fuckin' German
living in the Big House now. And just because you can't
lord it over people any more, big words. And big and all
as they are, you haven't a good word to say about
anything. Fuck you: What're you talking about?

Henry (*simply*)   Precisely.

Finbar   Ooh! precisely, ex-actly. Fuck you: Who d'you
think you are?

Henry (*simply*)   I wish to God I knew. And not much
chance of finding out: It is, as you have said, a most
distressing country.

Finbar (*containing his rage*)   I need – a *piss*. (*He is going out.*)

Henry   I'll come with you.

Finbar   What?! What?! You think you have all the
answers? She's my ride. (*And a harsh laugh?*)

Henry   Then we both like her – Yes we do. And there is
an abundance of her in it. And she is not going to save for
one – 'tis patently clear – what one cannot possibly use up.

Shh, she's back!

And **Vera** *comes in swinging a bottle/s by her side. She has changed and done herself up. The dress is makeshift but it creates the effect she wants: The marks of a whore and sexy.*

Vera   Okay, boys, show me what you've got.

Henry   Your mother's? (*The dress.*)

Vera   Yeh. D'you like it?

Henry   Mm!

Vera   My property. (*Turns to* **Finbar** *for his opinion of her body and dress:*) Hmm?

Finbar *is a mixture of fear and attraction: To stay or to go.*

Henry   We were only this minute discussing your property and reached impasse. So would you care to declare which of us you're going to have or shall we let the contest in drink continue 'til it's decided?

Vera   (*assesses them in turn. Then*)   It's my birthday!

Finbar   It's not – What? – Is it? (*And, confused, goes out.*) Fuckin'!

A telephone – on the floor somewhere? – starts ringing.

Henry   The drums (*phone*) have started, they have heard we are in occupation.

Vera   (*pelvic thrust – direction of phone or window*)   Font of love: Who's first?

Henry   Are you going to answer it?

Vera   No. They're going to have to arrive in person. I want to see them. *Here.* They *will* arrive, won't they?

Henry   The drums continue for three days, I believe: then they attack.

Vera   And I've bolted the door. Because when they arrive they're going to have to break it down to get in here. Just like what had to be done to my grandmother's house.

Only, I won't be on the floor. Then, as regards this place (*The hotel.*) I'll do – (*Shrugs:*) something. But it'll be clean, final.

Henry We are hopelessly outnumbered – And Finbar will desert: His nerve is cracking. They captured him once before and tortured him. But depend on me: I'll keep two rounds: They'll take neither of us alive.

Finbar (*making a tentative return*) Happy birthday, Vera!

Vera *and* **Henry** *start laughing.*

Vera Finbar, you old ponce, come to mama!

Henry (*pouring drinks – welcoming*) Nickerdepazze!

Finbar (*coming to join them*) I'm not taking my clothes off in front of him.

More laughter. And the phone is ringing again.

Finbar Nickerdepazze!

Henry Nickerdepazze!

Vera Let's *start* the party. (*A toast:*) Nickerdepazze!

Scene Seven

A table and four chairs (as in the bay of a window): **Tom**'*s house.*

Caitriona, **Tom**'*s wife, stands there (upstage) in forgotten purpose, a glass of water in her hand. She is pretty, petite. Long dress: Arab-type, perhaps, with the bodice done in coloured threads and beads. Now, a slow movement – a delayed reaction – to a noise off.* (**Tom** *letting himself in with his keys.*)

And **Tom** *comes in (leaving the door, off, open). He is upset and he starts to snivel. (No acknowledgement of* **Caitriona**.)

Caitriona (*upstage of him*), *unmoved, watching him, sidelong. A slow movement of her fist to her mouth: pills. And washing them down with water.*

The doorbell rings and **Mary Jane** *marches in (leaving the door, off, open). Briefest of greetings.*

Mary Jane   Caitriona.

Tom   I never thought I'd ... (*He is blowing his nose.*)

Mary Jane   How do we stop this?

Tom   Treasure, door please.

Caitriona *goes out, closes the door, returns in a moment.*

Mary Jane   It's a circus.

Tom   I never thought I'd ...

Mary Jane   What're we going to do?

Tom   Can we get you anything?

Mary Jane   Glass of water.

Tom   Little Treasure, glass of water for Mary Jane.

Caitriona *goes.*

Mary Jane   What action? (*Do we take.*)

Tom   I never thought I'd live to see a day like this.

Mary Jane (*to herself*)   Wonderful. And Henry Locke-Browne: That parasite.

Tom (*to himself*)   No. No. (*He refuses to call his brother-in-law a parasite.*) But he'll peter out.

Mary Jane   I know he will *peter* out, I know his form. Are you saying that we wait until she peters out, see what *she's* going to do next? O-Toole, Ve-rah!

Tom   I left word on the way home for Father Billy.

Mary Jane   *Why*! are you bringing priests into it, what use are *they*?

Tom   It's their flaming business, Mary Jane!

Mary Jane   They've been extraordinarily quiet about it for the past six and a half days!

Tom Father Billy Houlihan is a personal friend of the family, Mary Jane, and a personal friend of mine! I don't know *yet* what we can do: That's what we're here to find out.

Mary Jane How do *we* stand?

Tom Head. (*His hand to his head: He has a headache.*)

Mary Jane The situation of the auction is now totally confused in the eyes of the public: The auction is no longer a foregone conclusion: So where does that leave our arrangement?

Tom We have a deal.

Mary Jane It would give me *peace* to be shut of this.

Tom When I get the hotel, *the* Wool Stores are yours, to develop or expand or . . . What're you going to do with them?

Mary Jane The Wool Stores are just sitting there.

Tom Prime position. When I get the hotel *the* Wool Stores are yours for nothing.

Mary Jane *Sell* them to me.

Tom I never go back on a deal.

Mary Jane I've-done-every-thing-I-can for you!

Tom As a sister should.

Mary Jane As a sister should and as a brother would, sell the pff-wretched – sheds – to me! –

The doorbell is ringing –

Name your price! –

Tom (*calling*) Caitriona! –

Mary Jane And I'll see if I can meet it!

Tom Treasure!

Mary Jane Is there an ashtray in the house – glass of water?

Tom Simmer down. (*To room door to meet his guests.*)

Mary Jane (*to herself*) Geesstupid! (*Producing cigarettes.*)

Father Billy (*off*) Caitriona! How are you! Sure you're grand!

Tom Father!

Father Billy (*off*) Tom!

Tom Come in, come in!

Mary Jane (*lighting cigarette; to herself*) Wonderful!

Father Billy (*coming in*) Where did you get the gorgeous dress, Caitriona?

Marcia, *pushcar and* **Norman**, **Father Billy** *and*
Caitriona *are coming in.*
Marcia's *face is bloated from crying. She is angry, too: She has
stopped* **Norman** *from going to school.*
Father Billy *is reluctant to become involved in the O'Tooles'
problem. He is big-chested and broad-shouldered. (***Finbar***'s opinion
of him – later – about his being a secret body-builder is probably
right.) Edge of white silk scarf inside the collar of his waisted
overcoat. He is a nice, uncomplicated man and celibacy causes him no
problems. He is mostly aware of people using him but he cannot do
much about it but laugh and clap his hands.*

Father Billy (*announcing it*) We arrived together – And
the baby! Mary Jane!

Tom You're very good, Father.

Father Billy Oh now! Norman, and are you not at
school?

Marcia He's not.

Father Billy And are you sick?

Marcia He's not.

Tom Come in – Welcome! – I'll take your coat –
Treasure!

Father Billy No, I can only stay a minute, Tom – And what age is she now, Marcia?

Marcia Four months, Father.

Father Billy Four months, Baby Carol!

Caitriona (*suddenly*) Welcome one and all! How are you, Mary Jane!

Mary Jane I'm fine, Caitriona – Glass of water please?

Tom A glass of water, Treasure, for Mary Jane, and Father Billy would like?

Father Billy No, no, no, Tom, thanks! I – Caitriona, if you're going out to . . .

Caitriona (*drifting out of the room*) I am the doctor's daughter!

Father Billy If she's gone out for tea or –

Tom Would you like a drop? (*Of tea.*)

Father Billy Oh, tea, now, stop!

Tom *laughs heartily.*

Mary Jane We sit down? (*She sits/she is already seated.*)

Father Billy Is she all right, like? (**Caitriona**)

Tom Dr Kelly has her on a new course of pills.

Father Billy And she's responding.

Tom If these ones don't work he'll sign her in somewhere he said. (*Indicating where she should sit:*) Marcia.

Father Billy Oh well now, please God it won't come to that.

Marcia (*turns on* **Norman**) Run out in the garden and play! You're becoming too old-fashioned entirely! (**Norman** *goes. Bridling herself before she sits:*) No, he's *not* going to school!

Tom   Sit here, Father. (*Centre chair, a carver.*)

Father Billy   No! That seat belongs to the man of the
house, this is my seat. The old nerves (**Caitriona**'*s*) can be
the boyos. (*Sits.*) Well now, the gang's all here.

Marcia *starts crying.*

Father Billy   Oh, sure, now, like. (*He contains a sigh. And:*)
What's the latest?

Tom   It's becoming serious.

Mary Jane   It's *becoming* serious? The car is out of
control!

Marcia   I only want Henry to come home.

Mary Jane   And it's been going on now for six and a
half days and *people* in authority are standing idly by.

Father Billy   But what can *we* do, Mary Jane? These
aren't like the old days.

Mary Jane   *Nothing* can be done? Wonderful. For
inexplicable reasons our sister arrived home from America
six and a half days ago: For inexplicable reasons she then
went to live – In sin? – in the New Estate with someone
everyone here knows to be of questionable, dangerous and
proven disreputable character – let's not beat about any
bush – who is up to every deceit, graft, double-dealing,
confidence trick in the book to put it mildly. We tried, we
failed, to make civilised contact with her –

Tom   She nearly – (*Took the nose off him in the door.*)

Mary Jane   Shall I or shall you?

Marcia   Vera wants everything.

Mary Jane   Two and a half days ago she moved into the
hotel, breaking a back window – we found out about the
back window half an hour ago – to do so. (*For*) Two and a
half days every window in the hotel has been lit up, day
and night, the middle of the town, with our sister,
brother-in-law and one Mr Reilly parading themselves in all

manners of drunkenness, undress, unseemly behaviour in those same windows for all or any outside who cared to stand in the Square and watch. Now, are four grown people sitting here at this table – including myself – telling me that nothing can be done about it? I find this extraordinary. Are there no laws – ones of decency perhaps? – statutory, common, moral, to be enacted or observed? What other society, town, civilised country would put up with it?

Tom   I's lunacy.

Mary Jane   This morning then – Well, what were people to think when they started to assemble for more of the continuing show? The lights still on in every window but no sign or trace of life from them in there any more, no answer to the doorbell, phone, knocks on the door – what were people to think? Were they dead?

Tom   Send for the guards, send for an ambulance.

Marcia   I could roast her, I could scald her –

Tom   Marcia –

Marcia   She wants everything –

Father Billy   Oh sure, now sure –

Tom   There's no point in getting angry –

Marcia   I'd stick a knife in her, Father!

Tom   Marcia!

Father Billy   . . . Ambulance?

Tom   Ambulance.

Mary Jane   Half an hour ago –

Marcia   Henry is only trying to help.

Mary Jane   Half an hour ago we get our second call from the police –

Tom   The guards are up to here (*Their necks.*) with her –

Mary Jane   Our second call in less than a week: Come up to the hotel immediately, try our keys in the front door –

Tom   Can we do nothing to protect her from herself! –

Mary Jane   We tried our keys –

Tom   Ambulance waiting –

Mary Jane   But it was bolted from inside –

Tom   Locked.

Mary Jane   So – (*Gestures: What else could they do?*) We nodded to them to go ahead.

Tom   Break in the door, Father, force it.

Mary Jane   The humiliation. That's the present situation – the *latest*!

Father Billy   . . . But they were all right?

Mary Jane   Pfff! (*Dismisses his question.*)

Father Billy   But you went in. Did you not go in?

Mary Jane   We did *not* go in!

Marcia   The guards and Dr Kelly went in.

Mary Jane   That's what Vera wanted us to do!

Father Billy   (*is shocked that they did not go in*)   But they were all right?

Mary Jane   I know her!

Marcia   They'd fallen asleep, Father.

Mary Jane   Asleep?! – She wants a bigger scene –

Marcia   } They were asleep, they weren't doing a thing –

Mary Jane   } Well she's not having it! And don't forget I know Henry Locke-Browne too –

Marcia   } They were asleep! –

Tom } Marcia! –

Marcia } They weren't doing anything –

Mary Jane } Well, now that the police and Dr Kelly have woken them up –

Tom } Marcia! –

Marcia } How dare you, Mary Jane Mansfield, insinuate that my husband would –

Mary Jane } They're up and at it again!

Marcia } How dare you! How dare you! (*Crying again:*) How dare you.

Tom } Marcia!!!

Father Billy Oh sure, now sure. It isn't nice to see families fighting. (*He looks at his watch.*)

Mary Jane (*looks at him*) And that's it?

Father Billy Well, now, please God, we'll sort something out, like. I'll go up – (*He looks at his watch.*) – Oh I will, I'll go up there later on, this afternoon maybe, and ... (*He rises.*) But you'll have to excuse me now.

Mary Jane (*so much for*) People in authority.

Tom (*a reprimand*) There is much work remaining to protect the Catholic ethos in this country, Father Billy.

Father Billy Oh sure, there is. And I know it's upsetting, but what'll I say to her?! D'you see my point? Not like the old days, what! And whatever I say to her, will-she-listen?! (*And he laughs and claps his hands.*) What?

Mary Jane Nothing can be done? Fine.

Marcia (*venomously*) I'd lock her up!

The reaction to this is mild: Perhaps they have found the solution.

Father Billy Well, you understand that I have to be going.

Tom *rises and sees* **Father Billy** *to the door of the room.*

Tom   Caitriona! Father Billy is leaving! Treasure!

Father Billy *(going out)*   God bless you all now. I'll go up to them, Tom, I will, later on, and –

Tom   You're very good.

Father Billy *(off)*   Gorgeous dress, Caitriona! God bless, God bless . . .

The silence has continued at the table except for **Marcia**'s *sniffling.* **Tom** *returns to his chair.*

Tom   This needs thought. What did you say, Marcia?

Marcia *(weeping)*   I only want Henry to come home.

Tom   What did she say, Mary Jane?

Mary Jane   Insanity.

Tom   I's, yes, lunacy.

Mary Jane   She needs a shock.

Tom   Marcia?

Mary Jane   She needs a good fright.

Marcia *(venomously)*   Lock her up and maybe they'd keep her in there for ever! And it wouldn't be the first or the last time that that's what people have to do!

Mary Jane   Because – Who knows?! – what she is going to do next.

Tom   She needs care?

Marcia   And, no more than if it were Caitriona, you only need Dr Kelly's signature – one signature – to do it.

Mary Jane   Because she will never be content. Never.

Caitriona *comes in with a glass of water.*

Caitriona   Now. A glass of water shall we say.

Mary Jane   Thank you.

Caitriona   Smashing weather again thank God for the time of year. (*And she goes out again.*)

Mary Jane   Are we agreed? (*They are agreed.*) Now, there is one other issue. The hotel has to be withdrawn from auction: With all this confusion anyone, frankly, in the country would bid against you.

Tom*'s concerned face nods,* **Marcia** *weeps,* **Mary Jane** *takes a sip from her glass of water.*

Mary Jane   Let us not be sentimental: when she comes out – as-out-she-will-come – let us be prepared for her.

Scene Eight

Late afternoon. A double bed, a chair, a window: Hotel bedroom. (Items of clothing strewn about.)

Vera *and* **Finbar** *are in bed, and* **Henry** *too – or perhaps he is seated on the side of the bed. Various degrees of undress. There's something light-headed about them, bouts of uncontrollable giggling-laughter, 'morning-after-the-party' kind of stuff – and caused by the guards' and Dr Kelly's breaking-in.*

Vera*, though, is frustrated – and growing impatient: Her situation continues unresolved. She is leaning over herself, her head in her hands.* **Finbar** *is sitting up, cocky, celebratory. In a moment, he will lean out of the bed for the butt of a cigarette and to pick up a string, on which are a couple of medals, to loop it around his neck. And* **Henry** *– his shoulder-shaking fits of the giggles and a few gestures apart – is immobilised.*

As the lights come up:

Finbar   'Hullo?' (*Rural accent of guard.*)

Giggling-laughter.

Vera   No!

Finbar   . . . Do we have, Vera, any more cigarettes?

Vera   No!

Finbar   I always did a line in medals. I played with them in the cradle, I sold medals with my mother.

Vera   Where are they, do they exist, are they real? (**Tom** *and* **Mary Jane**.)

Finbar   Lord have Mercy on the soul of the woman.

Vera (*to* **Henry**)   No! (*He has held out his hand: He would dearly love a drink.*)

Finbar   And they're clean and you won't break your back carrying them anywhere. And you can bless them yourself.

Vera   Why didn't they come in when the guards and Dr Kelly broke in?

Finbar   'Hullo?'

More giggling.

Vera   No!

Finbar   You can sue the guards for the damage to the door. Fuckin' red-necks: 'Hullo?': Mouth on the first fella like the top of a hot-water bottle.

Renewed giggling.

Vera   No. I'm annoyed. (*Gets out of bed:*) What do I have to do to get them here?

Finbar   But it was clear for all to see they expected to find us in a coma at the least.

Vera   That wasn't how it was meant to have happened. (*She goes to the window.*)

Finbar   And Dr Kelly: 'Open your eyes. Can you hear me?'

Vera   I want to see them, I want to see their eyes.

Finbar   Aw but Jesus, Vera waking up! Scattered them! (**Vera**'s *sitting up suddenly out of her sleep, frightened of the guards and Dr Kelly.*)

Vera, *unlike the others, isn't laughing any more. She has come to a decision: 'Okay'. Into action: She finds a bundle of dresses – goes off* *for them? – to select one, and/or to abandon the idea in favour of simply putting on her mackintosh over whatever she is wearing. Next, she is looking around for something – an 'invitation brick', etc.*

Vera (*to herself*)   Okay. Where'd you leave the car?

Finbar   Just around the – (*Corner.*)

Vera   Car keys.

Finbar   What?

Vera   Car keys! I've a short run to do. I have to move – I need air – I have to get away. Annoyed, annoyed, annoyed, annoyed, annoyed! (*Collects her car keys.* **Finbar** *has reached out of the bed for his trousers for the keys.*) And the money.

Finbar   What?

Vera   Look!!! Just give it to me! – No old plámás (*bullshit*) – the money you stole from my wallet, I'm not saying a thing: there is nothing wrong with stealing. (*And while he gets the money for her, she is looking around for something:*) What am I looking for? A calling-card, an *invitation*-card.

A gesture from **Henry**, *this time to restrain/warn her from going out.*

No, something has started, I want it finished, I'm not waiting.

Finbar   Is the party over? (*Giving her the money.*)

Vera   No, the party isn't over yet: One more to finish it. I'd like them to attend me here for an occasion. Maybe an invitation-*brick* through Tom's window will do the trick: Better still – bigger window! – Mary Jane's supermarket is only down there: I'll walk (*In answer to another gesture from* **Henry**:) No! If you're up, dressed, I'll unlock – the cellars! – when I get back. This'll only take a second (*And she's gone, purposefully.*)

Finbar (*swings his legs out of the bed*)   I couldn't give a shite! (*Finds his underpants under the sheets, puts them on:*) Do you smoke after you've had intercourse? Well, she said, I never looked. (*To the window:*) Look at her striding! Oh, 'Hullo?': the red-necks are down there, your man with the mouth. Look at them watching her. (*Dressing through the following:*) But from my knowledge – well, you're meant to be the expert – they can't touch you on your own property. Or where you're a guest they can't. Unless you're dead of course. That's why they didn't lay a finger on us earlier. Though you could see they wanted to. Aw Jesus, Henry, get ready, she'll be back in a second. (*He finds* **Henry**'s *shoes and dumps them at his feet:*) But you're some man for it all right, I have to hand it to you, the way you can carry it.

Henry, *slow mechanical movements, dressing.*

Finbar I never had such a nice few days! (*To the window again:*) The red-necks are gone. Somewhere . . . Father Billy Houlihan. Is he considering coming in? No. Great pair of shoulders on him. I'd say he's a secret body-builder, would you say? No, I never had such a nice few days. Still, d'you ever give any thoughts to reincarnation? If I have any say in the matter I'm going to ask to be let back as a dog. A greyhound. I know it's only a toy they're after but the way that they go after it. Beautiful. Pure. (*He's dressed, ready.*) She (**Vera**) should be coming back.

The lights are fading a little. They continue to fade.

What? (*Why isn't* **Vera** *returned.*) . . . No but, we were talking there: I'll tell *you* one. And this was only last year. But I was giving a man a hand to dig a grave. An aul' one out there in Bungesh side that'd died. Grave dug, we're putting her down, a voice from the back. 'Take her up! That's *my* plot of land!' May I drop down dead here myself this minute if I tell a lie. And why did he wait till the grave was dug? We had to dig another! . . . Unless she (**Vera**) met someone? (*Still looking out the window; absently.*) Take her up, that's my plot of land.

Henry My mother once told me that all babies cry at their first view of the sea.

Finbar (*absently; to himself*) What?

Henry Lord have mercy on the soul of the woman. But in my case, when she took me to see it, I laughed. (*He's dressed.*)

Finbar (*dejected; not listening; disappointed that* **Vera** *has not returned*) D'you love me she said, do I love you he said, amn't I riding you.

Henry They've got her.

Finbar What?

Henry They are unbeatable. But put yourself in my hands: You and I together shall take the matter and our custom to Mannions of the Hollow.

Scene Nine

Upstairs sitting-room in the hotel. (It is three and a half days later.)

Vera *comes in with a pair of candlesticks and candles. She is sober and in a simple dress. The room has been arranged (by her) as for an occasion. A table has been added (the one she adverted to in Scene Six.) The dust-sheet has been removed from the piano: she puts the candlesticks on it. Drinks, formally arranged, wait. Civilisation.*

Doorbell, off, downstairs. A beat. And she calls:

Vera It's open!

And **Father Billy** *comes up and in.*

Father Billy It's only me.

She waits for more, as from one who has been sent on a message.

Father Billy They're on their way. Well, (*they're*) sitting in the car out there for a minute, having a chat. So ... (*He is not at ease.*) They suggested that I be here, but if you'd prefer? (*That he should leave.*)

Vera Open house.

Father Billy Because you'll have business to discuss.

Vera No, there will be no business discussed. (*Which is a surprise for* **Father Billy**.) What would you like?

Father Billy Ah no sure.

Vera Do.

Father Billy Well . . . is that Tropicana?

Vera That is Tropicana. (*She pours for him.*)

Father Billy I love Tropicana. It's from Florida. But you're doing the right thing, asking them nicely to visit after all the, all the – Thanks, thank you, God bless! All the comuffle.

Vera Sit down.

Father Billy It was a mistake – They know it – having you put into that place.

Vera Maybe not. (*Which is a bigger surprise for* **Father Billy**.) Sit down, Father.

Father Billy But it's a blessing that you're well again and that they let you out.

Vera And is everything well with you?

Father Billy Why wouldn't it! I told them you're calm. (*After a beat, impulsively:*) I *hate* trouble, Vera, I *hate* it.

Vera There will be no trouble.

Father Billy We'll say no more.

Vera And did you find Henry and Finbar?

Father Billy I did. But they're . . . (*Drunk.*) Maybe they'll come.

Vera Thank you.

The doorbell rings.

Vera It's open!

Father Billy That'll be them now . . . Here they are now.

Mary Jane, **Marcia**, **Caitriona**, **Norman** *and* **Tom** *are coming in: Varying degrees of self-consciousness. (***Mary Jane***, now, seeming to treat the past events as if they were a joke; ***Marcia*** resentful but instructed to contain herself; ***Caitriona***, 'responding' to the pills but cranky; ***Norman*** has been told what to say; ***Tom*** looking both enthusiastic and fearful at the idea of meeting ***Vera*** . . .)*

Father Billy   Look who's here!

Mary Jane   How yeh!

Father Billy   And Marcia!

Mary Jane   How yeh? (*Coming to shake hands.*)

Father Billy   Wonderful!

Vera   Mary Jane.

Mary Jane   We didn't have to break the door down this time!

Marcia *is shaking hands with* **Vera**.

Vera   Marcia.

Mary Jane   Oh boy is it a crazy world!

Caitriona   How the hell are you, Vera!

Vera   Caitriona.

Father Billy   That's it!

Vera   Norman?

Father Billy   Isn't he getting big?

Norman   Welcome home, Auntie Vera!

Vera   Thank you.

Father Billy   That's the man!

Tom   Lookit! (*Hoarsely, emotional, his hand out but his feet are stuck to the floor.*)

Vera *goes to him and shakes hands with him.*

Father Billy   Lovely hurling, girl!

Tom   I couldn't be! (*He couldn't be happier about anything.*)

Caitriona   Up on your bike! (*Strident.*)

Tom   (*turns on her to reprimand her but, instead, laughs heartily, and*)   Gas woman!

Vera   – *a gesture* – *invites them to sit down.*

Mary Jane   Well, you're looking well – considering! Are you?

Vera   (*'Yes'*)   Sit down.

Mary Jane   We won't stay. We got your – summons – and we are only popping in. We all do things, mistakes frankly, when we are heated. The situation got out of control, there was the medical opinion, among the other factors, and – oh boy is it one crazy world and do we all contribute to it! And we're sorry. Now, Tom has a suggestion.

Vera   You won't stay? (*She's surprised; she doesn't like it.*)

Tom   Tomorrow, Vera: If we could meet in the solicitor's office?

Vera   That won't be possible. I'm eager to get back to the States, clear up the rest of my act, start new.

Tom   But.

Mary Jane   When?

Vera   What?

Mary Jane   Might you?

Vera   Go back to the States? First thing in the morning . . . If not sooner.

Mary Jane   Well, in that case. Where would you like us to sit?

Vera   Anywhere.

Tom   Where are *you* sitting, Vera?

Vera   Anywhere.

Father Billy   Yes, do, sit and we'll have a chat.

Tom   This was mam's chair. Not joining the circle, Treasure?

Caitriona   Here? – Here? – Where exactly would you like me to sit?

Mary Jane   I see you've resurrected the table?

Tom   The deals that were done across this table, Mary Jane!

*At this point, **Vera** is lighting a candle. What is she up to, they wonder. She lights the second candle.*

Father Billy   But d'you know who I love? Esther Williams. D'you know her, Caitriona, d'you, Marcia?

Tom   The swimmer, Father?

Father Billy   The film star sure! I switched on the telly last night and there she was. But you don't see much of her any more: I wonder why is that, like?

Tom   Wouldn't she be getting on now, Father?

Father Billy   Aw she wouldn't be that old! What? (*They are not sure what age Esther Williams might be.*) . . . But the film was called *Dangerous When Wet*. Dangerous when wet, what! I looked it up in the papers. Where Esther has to swim the Channel. She's called Annie in the film, Annie Higgins, like, I think. I think maybe she was meant to be Irish. I wonder? 'Cause I missed the beginning. I wouldn't say it was one of her best because I've seen a few of them. But there was a French lassie in it too. Denise? Denise? Denise Darcel! Oh, a bit of a lady! And says Denise to Esther: 'You sweem ze Chan-nel and you mebbe win ze med-al, but that won't kip you warm at night.' You never saw, Caitriona, *Dangerous When Wet*, Marcia?

Marcia   No, Father.

Vera   Now, what can I get everyone – Caitriona?

Caitriona   What's it like being locked up?

Vera   . . . Oh. (*She doesn't want to talk about it.*)

Father Billy   Oh but it was well done!

Caitriona   But what's it like?

Tom   She told you –

Caitriona   She didn't! They had you locked up in a mental home – How was it?

Vera   I've put it behind me, Caitriona. Marcia?

Marcia   Port!

Caitriona   She's put it where?

Tom   Treasure –

Caitriona   But there's nothing wrong with her!

Tom   Little Treasure –

Caitriona   Is she mad? – Are you mad? –

Tom   Haven't we talked about it enough? –

Caitriona   She's been locked up for three days –

Mary Jane   Caitriona!

Caitriona   D'you mind?! I'm interested in these matters! Did they find anything wrong with you?

Vera   No.

Caitriona   Did they find anything wrong with you, find anything wrong with you, did they?

Vera   No.

Caitriona   They found nothing wrong with her!

Tom } Caitriona!

Mary Jane } Caitriona!

Caitriona   I rest my case.

Vera *hands port to* **Marcia**.

Father Billy　Love Esther.

Vera　What would you like, Mary Jane?

Caitriona　So why did they keep you in for three days?

Vera　Three and a half. (*To herself:*) Okay. (*She has decided
to talk.*) It was awful. (*To* **Caitriona**:) I had to wait my
turn for the psychiatrist. But I used the time. Well, why
not: To think about this place (*the hotel*): How much it
meant to you, and what did it mean to me. And how did I
come to find myself in, well, a loony bin. That I've been in
a bit of a state since I came home. In a bit of a state for a
long time. Well, I mean, I've been praying for a long time
now for the grace that would change me, conform me,
make me worthy. I used to think I was real because I came
from here.

Mary Jane　Yes, Vera, we know about – (*All that kind of
stuff.*)

Vera　And all that American jazz (**Mary Jane**). Then
the psychiatrist: We had a great talk. A test. But he gave
me this. (*Producing a slip of paper:*) A little fella. He wrote it
down: that I'm not a threat to myself or to anyone else,
and that I'm capable of making decisions. And I've made
them. (*She offers the slip of paper for their inspection. They do not
'need' to see it.*) So, I'm the only certified sane person in the
room. And that the reason I came home in the first place,
I told him, was to pay my respects to an old woman, my
grandmother, who was the nearest in family or friend
anyone could hope for: That I hadn't quite paid my
respects but that when – *if* – I got out I would finalise the
matter. And that's all that remains to be done.

The reason for **Vera**'*s coming home is news to* **Mary Jane** *and*
Tom.

Mary Jane　The reason, Vera, why you weren't informed
sooner about grandmother's death was because we were all
upset.

Father Billy   May she rest in peace.

Vera (*a slight nod acknowledges* **Father Billy**; *impassive previously to* **Mary Jane**)   So what would everyone like? Tom?

Tom   Well, d'you know what I'm going to say to you? A bit of openness is all I want. You don't have to go to any solicitor's office: We'll do it across this table.

Vera   Ahmmm!

Tom   You don't understand me! I don't think you'll be disappointed in our proposition. Daddy sitting there ('*Man dear alive*'!) What used he say? You can get nothing for nothing!

Vera   You can.

Tom *opens his mouth to speak –*

Vera   I won't discuss it across any table. I've decided what to do with the hotel.

Tom   What?

Vera   You'll have to wait and see.

Mary Jane   Relax, Tom.

Vera   Finalise, bury everything and mark the occasion by our getting together. Now, is that not possible?

Mary Jane   Open the wine, pass round the pipes, call the fiddler! Vera gets her way again! (*She starts to pour drinks.*)

Vera (*takes a Coke to* **Norman**)   We've been neglecting you.

Tom (*to* **Mary Jane**)   What?

Mary Jane   A Jemmy for Tom! – (*Jameson whiskey. To him.*) Play along with her –

Father Billy   Now, Marcia – (*Another port.*)

Mary Jane   Father Billy is all right –

Father Billy   Oh now! –

Mary Jane   With his camouflaged drink! And would you like a song, Vera?

Father Billy   Did you hear that, Marcia, a song!

Caitriona   'Summertime an' the livin' is easy . . .'

Tom   'Fish are jumpin –' Coke for Treasure!

Mary Jane (*aside to* **Tom**)   Relax. (*To herself:*) She's a fool.

Father Billy   This is more like it!

Vera   And for yourself, Mary Jane?

Mary Jane   Oh what the hell, life is short! (*She has a whiskey.*)

Tom   Well? (*Glass raised: A toast.*)

Father Billy   To God and St Patrick! (*Laughing.*) –

Tom   And to our native land! (*Laughing.*)

Vera   To the dead!

And as they drink, **Caitriona**'s *toast:*

Caitriona   Prozac! (*And singing again to herself:*) 'Summertime and the livin' is easy . . .'

Off, downstairs, the doorbell.

Tom   This's what we should have done last week –

Vera (*calls*)   Come in! –

Tom   Six months, a year ago!

Doorbell.

Caitriona   'Your daddy's rich . . .'

Henry (*off*)   Let down the bridge!

Father Billy   That'll be Henry, like –

Vera   Push!

Marcia Let him in! (*Alarm.*)

Caitriona 'So hush little baby . . .'

Father Billy And Finbar.

Vera (*to* **Tom** *who has been asking her would she like him to answer the door*) Open house!

Tom (*going out*) This's more like it!

Marcia He hasn't been home in a week. And now he's sleeping up in that dirty fella's dirty house.

And, during the above, **Henry** *appears to have discovered that the door was open: He is on the stairs. (He is very drunk but he is straight-backed; he knows very well where he is; despair behind his attempted panache. And* **Finbar** *appears to be reluctant – wary at first – about joining the group.)*

Henry (*off*) Finbar, you can make it! –

Tom (*off*) Henry! –

Henry (*off*) There is water beyond this rise: I am sure of it! (*He comes in.*)

Tom (*off*) Come on up, Finbar! –

Henry I have nothing to declare but my schizophrenia!

Marcia He's killing himself.

Henry (*to* **Father Billy**, *as to a barman*) Same again!

Marcia He's like a tramp.

Henry (*to the four women, equally*) How are you, how are you, how are you, how are you! (*Nothing to* **Norman** *though* **Norman** *is clearly visible to him.*)

Father Billy How are you, Henry boy!

Henry Ah! – (*As if only now recognising who* **Father Billy** *is.*) – he comes with garlic and crucifix.

Tom (*coming in with* **Finbar**) Come in, my friend, and take off your coat!

Father Billy   How are you, Finbar boy!

Tom   And any friend of any sister of mine is good enough for me! Come over here beside Vera.

Finbar *favours / will favour a place near* **Henry**.

Henry   What did I tell you: Water! (*The drinks.*)

Father Billy   One more (*drink*) isn't going to matter at this stage.

Tom   Two gas men! Where were we, Vera?

Henry   'Breeng flowers of the rarest . . .' (*Singing; eyes shut.*)

Caitriona   'Summertime an' the livin' . . .' (*Joining in competition.*)

Father Billy (*laughing*)   One voice! –

Tom (*laughing*)   One voice! Treasure! – Henry! (*For silence.*) Lookit, I feel! (*He feels great.*) Is there anyone here has any serious objections to a decent song?!

Father Billy   Now you're talking!

Tom   Do you, Vera?

Vera   On the contrary.

Henry   Lovely!

Mary Jane   Marcia will sing.

Father Billy   Marcia! Misty!

Tom   Folks! –

Mary Jane   Now's your chance, Marcia! –

Tom   I give you –

Caitriona   Folks! – (*Bad and cranky mimicry of* **Tom**.)

Tom   I crave silence for! Mrs Henry Locke-Browne!

Mary Jane   . . . Ah come on!

Father Billy   She will.

Tom   This is a night for reconciling families.

Mary Jane   Sing!

And **Marcia** *sings. And, whatever her propensity for distress, she is a good singer, it's her song. Indeed, in what follows (and though there is an element of prostitution in what they are doing) they succumb to their own songs and show/redeem something of their innocence.*

Vera*'s recurring 'Ah-haa!' is a complex of emotions: the sound of an afternoon girl in an afternoon bar pretending to be having a good time; at another level there is harshness in it as at having been betrayed, while at the same time there is a cry in it for the thing that has done the betraying; a modern olagon at a wake . . . (and it's a preparation for the flood-gates that open in the next scene.)*

There is ongoing pain in **Henry***'s repeated 'Lovely!' Unlike* **Vera***, who will escape,* **Henry** *is caught for ever. (Suicidal thoughts.)*

Finbar*, like the scavenger, dealing in the temporalities: free drink and a degree of self-congratulations about being included in and dealing with this company.*

Marcia   'Look at me, I'm as helpless as a kitten up a tree . . . I feel misty, I'm too much in love.'

Applause, together with:

Tom   Now who's the singer!

Mary Jane   Never fails.

Father Billy ⎫   Who is the singer, who is the singer!

Tom ⎭   Can she sing?!

Mary Jane ⎫   Never better.

Father Billy ⎭   My life on you, Marcia!

Tom   Who's next, Vera?

Finbar ⎫   Excellent, Mrs Locke-Browne!

Tom ⎭   Whose twist is it?

Vera   Yourself!

Tom What would you like?

Finbar Three-legged dog!

Henry Lovely!

Finbar Three-legged dog goes into this saloon yeh see and he has a look around: I'm lookin' for the man who shot my paw! Jesus!

Laughter / applause.

Mary Jane Jeekers! What is the world coming to?

Tom Gas, one gas man!

Henry Lovely!

Father Billy (*of* **Henry**) He'll be grand.

Tom (*to* **Vera**) Song? (*What song.*)

Vera The Lily of Killarney.

Tom ⎫ Aw! (*Laughing.*)

Father Billy ⎭ Aw! (*Laughing.*)

Tom Folks! –

Caitriona Folks! –

Father Billy The Moon Hath Raised – (*To the piano, to play.*)

Tom From the Lily *off* Killarney!

Henry Lovely!

Tom I feel like killing a flaming calf! (*And – his introduction played – he sings on cue:*) 'The moon hath raised her lamp above / To light the way to thee, my love / To light the way to thee, my love; / Her rays upon the waters play / To tell me eyes more bright than they / Are watching through the night / Are watching through the night. / I come, I come, my heart's delight / I come, I come, my heart's delight / I come, I come, my heart's delight / I come, I come, my heart's delight / I come, I come, my heart's delight.'

Father Billy (*playing and singing*) 'On hill and dale the moonbeams fall / And spread their silver light o'er all / But those bright eyes –'

Tom/Father Billy (*duet*) 'But those eyes I soon shall see / Reserve their glorious light for me / Reserve their glorious light for me / Reserve their glorious light for me; / Methinks that love they do invite / I come, I come, my heart's delight.'

Tom 'I come, my heart's delight'

Father Billy 'I come, I come, my heart's delight'

Tom 'I come, my heart's delight'

Father Billy 'I come, I come, my heart's delight'

Tom/Father Billy 'I come, my heart's delight, my heart's delight.'

Applause, together with:

Henry Lovely! –

Mary Jane Not bad! –

Vera Ah-haa!

Finbar Lovely, Father, lovely, Mr O'Toole!

Tom (*to* **Vera**) You're not going back in the morning! – 'Cause I won't let you!

Vera Ah-haa!

Father Billy Who's next?

Tom Folks! –

Caitriona Folks! –

Tom I had one good reason for getting my humble piece out of the way first –

Finbar Father, d'you know –

Tom   There's someone here I didn't want to follow –
Ciuinness (*quiet*) there a sec, Finbar – someone, who is not
only nothing short of being a brilliant musician, but
someone –

Mary Jane   We're in suspense! –

Tom   But someone who can sing a mean song: Father
Billy Houlihan!

Father Billy   Oh now!

Tom   And if there's a better organist in the whole country
I'd like to meet him.

Mary Jane   'Sea, oh the sea'!

Caitriona (*of her glass of Coke*)   This is piss.

Tom   Treasure! –

Caitriona   Sedimentary, my dear Watson!

Henry   The organ is a musical JCB!

Caitriona (*pouring vodka for herself*)   Does anyone here have
any serious objections to my taking a decent drink?

Henry   Lovely!

Caitriona   Cheers, everybody, cheers, Norman!

Tom (*winks at* **Vera** *and is introducing* **Father Billy**
again)   Father Billy!

Finbar (*singing*)   'When the golden sun sinks in the hill /
And the toil of a long day is o'er –'

Father Billy   Man, Finbar! –

Finbar   'Though the road may be long, with the lilt of a
song / I'll forget I was weary before'

Father Billy *comes in with accompaniment.*

Finbar   'Far away where the blue shadows fall / I shall
come to contentment and rest / And the toils of the day
will be all charmed away / In my little grey home in the
west'.

Father Billy (*speaking it, wanting the singer to get the proper tempo*) 'There are hands that will welcome me in'

Finbar 'There are lips I am burning to kiss / There are two eyes that shine'

Tom } 'Just because they are mine'

Finbar } 'Just because they are mine / And a thousand things others may miss / It's a corner of heaven itself —'

Henry Lovely! —

Finbar 'Yet it's only a tumble-down nest —' (*Momentary balk.*)

Father Billy (*providing the high note*) 'But —'

Finbar 'With love brooding there / There's no place can compare / To my little grey home in the west.'

Applause, together with:

Mary Jane Sentimental rubbish — My little grey home in the — Pfff! —

Caitriona What does anybody think of our politicians — Can we have a serious conversation? —

Mary Jane How are you, Henry!

Caitriona Aren't they the most — Have you ever come across —

Henry Lovely, Mary Jane! —

Caitriona Such an unhandsome bunch of flutes!

Tom Vera? (*Whose next?*)

Vera Mary Jane.

Mary Jane *Me?!*

Vera Vision of Connaught.

Mary Jane (*recites*) 'I walked entranced through a land of morn / The sun with wondrous excess of light shone down and glanced over seas of corn / And lustrous gardens a-left and right; / Even in the clime of resplendent Spain beams no such sun upon such a land; / But it was the time, 'twas in the reign of Cathal Mor of the Wine Red Hand!'

Tom (*rapt admiration*)   Shh-shh-shh for Mary Jane.

Mary Jane   Anon stood nigh by my side a man / Of princely aspect and port sublime / Him queried I, 'O my Lord and Khan! What clime is this and what golden time?' When he – (*She has grown self-conscious; dismisses it.*) Pff, rubbish!

Tom   No! –

Father Billy   No! –

Finbar   No, Mrs Mansfield!

Father Billy   Vision of Connaught –

Tom   It's lovely! – (*To* **Vera**:) Isn't it? –

Finbar   It is! –

Vera   Ah-haa! –

Father Billy   By James Clarence Mangan –

Tom   Him queried I!

Henry (*takes it up: Rising slowly but violent movement of his arms/fists, eyes shut*)   Him queried I, 'O my Lord and Khan! What clime is this, and what golden time?' – K.H.A.N., Khan, identical with the Irish, C.E.A.N.N., Ceann, head or chieftain. When he – 'The clime is a clime to praise, the clime is Erin's, the green and bland and it is the time, these be the days of Cathal Mor of the Wine Red –' Rubbish! A pen, anybody – anybody pen, piece of paper!?

*He has a pen and is given a piece of paper (***Vera***'s 'certificate'?) and he starts to write. (We shall get his composition later).*

Marcia   Then I saw thrones and circling fires!

Mary Jane   And a dome rose near me as by a spell /

Whence flowed the tones of silver lyres and many voices in
wreathed swell; / And their thrilling chime fell on my ears
as the heavenly hymn of an angel band – / 'It is now the
time, these be the years of Cathal Mor of the Wine Red
Hand!'

Henry (*writing*)   Lovely!

Marcia   I sought the hall!

Mary Jane   I sought the hall

Caitriona   And behold! – a change

Mary Jane   From light to darkness

Marcia   Joy to woe!

Mary Jane   Joy to woe. Kings, nobles, all

Caitriona ⎤   Looked aghast and strange

Marcia ⎦   Looked aghast and strange

Mary Jane   The minstrel group sat

Marcia   In dumbest show!

Mary Jane   Had some great crime wrought this dread
amaze, this

Caitriona   Terr-or?

Mary Jane   Terror

Marcia   None seemed to understand.

*A beat, the trio of performers smile at one another without knowing
why.*

Vera (*to herself*)   Ah-haa . . .

Marcia   I *again* walked forth –

Caitriona   But lo! –

Mary Jane   Lo! –

Marcia   Lo!

The three of them, now – frightening themselves with the poem – are giggling like schoolgirls, bobbing their heads together for a moment.

Mary Jane But lo! the sky showed fleckt with blood

Marcia And an alien sun

Caitriona Glared from the north

Mary Jane And there stood on high amid his shorn beams

Marcia } A Skel-et-on!

Caitriona ⌡ A Skel-et-on!

Tom (*whispers his enthusiasm to* **Vera**) Great!

Mary Jane A skeleton. (*And tosses off the rest of it:*) It was by a stream of the Castle Maine, one autumn eve in Teuton's land, that I dreamed this dream of the time and reign of . . . ?

All (*except* **Vera**) Cathal Mor of the Wine Red Hand.

And further drinks are poured as they applaud themselves, together with:

Father Billy There's learning for you! –

Henry (*writing*) Lovely! –

Finbar I hear a sudden cry of pain there is a rabbit in a snare! (*Which also means 'lovely!'*) –

Caitriona I am the doctor's daughter! (*Also means 'lovely!' She kisses* **Mary Jane***:*) Kiss-kiss!

Tom, *laughing – though his hand to his head: his recurring headache – has joined* **Vera**. **Mary Jane**, *now, to* **Vera***'s other side.* **Vera** *knows what they are up to. The three of them watching the rest of the party.*

Caitriona (*kissing people and wanting to be kissed. To* **Marcia**) Kiss-kiss!

Finbar But! – as Shakespeare'd say – more of this anon!

Father Billy No! No! I'm not allowed that, Caitriona! (*Meaning* **Caitriona**'s *kiss.*)

Caitriona Norman: Kiss-kiss! (*She kisses* **Norman** *and gets him another Coke.*)

Mary Jane Good idea of yours, Vera. (*The wake/the party.*)

Tom Good idea?! Magic! Isn't this what life is all about, isn't it?

Vera (*calls*) Another song!

Tom Lookit! is *she* going back in the morning, Mary Jane?

Mary Jane I don't know.

Tom (*to* **Vera**) Are you going back in the morning?

Vera Another song! –

Tom Well, you're going back over my dead body, my lady! Man dear alive sure! (*'This is what life is all about!'*) And the catching up we have to do! Wait'll you see how fast I'll be getting rid of this lot in a minute and the three of us'll sit down and finish that bottle together – What d'you say, Mary Jane?

Vera D'you have a headache, Tom?

Vera *had produced the phial of pills that we saw in Scene Five.* **Tom** *dismisses his headache: He is laughing heartily and pointing at* **Caitriona** *who is joining them:*

Caitriona Kiss-kiss!

Mary Jane I've had mine already, Caitriona!

Vera (*offering a pill to* **Tom**) Take one of these.

Caitriona (*kisses* **Tom**) Kiss-kiss. (*Turns to* **Vera**, *kisses her:*) I don't care what they say about you, I envy you. (*And pops the pill.*)

Vera (*offering him another pill*) Tom?

Tom You're very good. (*And he swallows it.*)

Mary Jane   What are they?

Vera (*extricating, removing herself from them*)   They're very effective. Let's finish the wake – Father Billy, 'Sea, oh the sea'!

Henry   Everybody! (*He stands.*)

Father Billy   Let him off.

Tom   Another limerick, Henry?

Henry   My dearest Marcia, by the time you read this I shall be no more.

Some laughter / recognition.

How can I explain what I do not understand myself. I am being unfaithful in going to sleep with death but have no thought in your mind that I was ever – ever – unfaithful to you in life. All my love to Norman and to Baby Carol. Yours, Henry Locke-Browne. (*He goes out to the gents.*)

Applause.

Mary Jane   That's a new version, Henry!

Finbar (*to himself*)   Fuckin'!

Caitriona   Lovely!

Father Billy (*of* **Henry**)   He'll be grand now for another six months.

Tom   In quick, Father, before someone else starts.

The lights are fading. **Father Billy** *is singing and playing a jazzy version of the ballad.*

Father Billy   I'd better because I've first Mass to say in the morning. 'The sea, oh the sea, gra geal mo croi, long may it roll between England and me . . .'

The lights are down, the music stops.

The lights come up. **Vera** *is pouring a careful – deliberate drink for herself.* **Tom** *and* **Caitriona** *are all but asleep in the couch;* **Caitriona** *is feeling amorous.* **Henry** *is back in his seat, head*

bowed over the table; **Marcia** *and* **Norman** *watch and wait;*
Finbar *seated; he is extremely drunk.* **Vera** *lights a cigarette.*

Father Billy *(off)*   Good night, God bless, Mary Jane!

Mary Jane *(off)*   Good night!

Caitriona   Bita nookey for Little Treasure.

Tom *giggles.*

Mary Jane *(returns)*   I'll see you out, Finbar.

Finbar   Is the party over?

Mary Jane *looks at* **Vera**.

Vera   Yeh.

Henry *(to himself, head bowed)*   Lovely.

Finbar   Permission to go to the cassie?

Norman *(nudged by* **Marcia***)*   Dad?

Finbar *(goes out to the gents)*   I hear a sudden cry of pain.

Norman   Dad?

Finbar *(off)*   Now I hear the cry again . . .

Henry *(finds a drink left behind by someone)*   Careless
shepherds leave a feast for the wolf. *(He knocks it back.)*

Marcia   Henry, I'm your wife. Are you coming home?

Henry *(to himself)*   Lovely, lovely . . . *(He is crying.)*

Tom *and* **Caitriona** *giggle in their sleep.*

Marcia *is assisting* **Henry** *to his feet. He declines her help and
gets up.*

Henry   Have you once – ever! – seen me stagger? I do
not permit it in myself.

He steps aside for **Marcia** *and* **Norman** *to precede him.*
Marcia, *bridling her shoulders in some private triumph she considers
she is having, leaves with* **Norman**. **Henry** *bows to the room and
follows.* **Vera** *blows out the candles, sits, gauging her drink as to*

when she wants to finish it. **Tom** *and* **Caitriona** *are asleep.*

Vera　They'll wake up ... What's it worth? (*The hotel.*)

Mary Jane　... What are you going to do?

Vera　I think you know, Mary Jane.

Mary Jane　... If it's what I think?

Vera　How is Declan?

Mary Jane　Holding the fort: we're open seven days a week ... You don't have to be so generous, you know.

Vera　It isn't worth a toss. (*She finishes her drink, collects her coat and bag.*)

Mary Jane　Vera.

Vera　We have nothing more to say to each other.

She leaves. **Mary Jane**'s *smile: She has got what she wants; smile beginning to question itself: Has she got what she wants? To the window to watch* **Vera** *(and to wait there for* **Vera**'s *car).*

Finbar (*off and coming in*)　I have one! Yeh see, yeh see, Jesus, Mary and Joseph are going down the road and they meet the good fairy, and the good fairy – Mrs Mansfield – the good fairy says to them anyway, think he says and I'll give you a wish, I'll give you one wish each but it can be anything you like, anything at all. I'd like says Jesus – he was first – I'd like says he to be thirty-four. And St Joseph was next. I'd like says St Joseph to have a child of my own ...

A car starting up in the night during this – **Vera**'s *car. Now the lights of the car washing the hotel, washing* **Mary Jane** *and* **Finbar** *in the window.*

Finbar　And the Blessed Virgin was last. I'd like says the Blessed Virgin, I'd like says Our Lady to go back to Mayo.

He laughs, highly amused. **Mary Jane** *hits him with her fist and leaves.* **Finbar** *staggering, reeling in laughter and pain.*

The sound of **Vera**'s *car continues.*

Scene Ten

An open space: A graveyard. Morning.

Mrs Conneeley, *overcoat as in Scene One, is moving about a space in the ground, a rectangle, a grave. She picks a weed. A car, off, approaching, which she does not register until it stops. She waits.*

And **Vera** *is coming in.*

Mrs Conneeley   You're on the road early!

Vera   Yeh!

Mrs Conneeley   Did you sell! (*Which is another greeting.*)

Vera (*laughs*)   No! I called to the house: Paddy said this is where you might be he thought.

Mrs Conneeley   Yes. This is where my husband is buried. It's getting crowded, Vera? (*The graveyard is.*) . . . You're on your way back?

Vera   I am. So! (*She flaps her hands to her sides.*) Your other son.

Mrs Conneeley   Francis?

Vera   Francis, solicitor. Where is he in Newcastle?

Mrs Conneeley   The Main Street. (*And, as in Scene Two, she is both surprised at and proud of* **Francis**'s *success.*)

Vera (*as if in easy dismissal of a matter*)   Nah, I didn't sell. But I'm going through Newcastle and I thought I'd call in on him. Something simple. Hmm? (*The 'Hmm?' may be silent, a look, as if she wants* **Mrs Conneeley**'s *support/approval of what she is going to do.*)

Mrs Conneeley   Yes?

Vera   Oh, I just want to – (*She shrugs.*) simply – sign over a place to my family. Clean. Final.

Mrs Conneeley (*nods. Then, the crowded graveyard again*)   . . . And I remember the day it was opened. The first person buried in it. He was a Kerrigan. They say he was forty. And in the same week, she would have been only eight or nine years old, one of the

O'Malleys below, Sally. And d'you know, those two held this place for a year.

Stoops to pick another weed. And **Vera** *does the same, assisting her.*

Mrs Conneeley   I never bothered to mark it. (*Dismissive:*) Ah, headstones! What is it but an aul' hole in the ground.

Vera   . . . I was thinking about what you were saying.

Mrs Conneeley   Hah? (*Can't remember.*)

Vera   Loneliness.

Mrs Conneeley   Oh! (*And she starts laughing.*)

And **Vera** *starts to laugh too. But now she is crying. Tears that she cannot stop, that she has been suppressing throughout. She begins to sob. Her sobbing continues, becoming dry and rhythmical: Grief for her grandmother, for the family that she perhaps never had, and for herself and her fear at this, her first acceptance of her isolation.*

Mrs Conneeley *puts her arms around her and holds her and lets her sob on. And* **Vera** *holds* **Mrs Conneeley**.

Vera's *tears are subsiding.* **Mrs Conneeley** *resumes the weeding.*

Mrs Conneeley   Yes . . . No, I never bothered to mark it. But it gets overgrown. And they're known to make mistakes, Vera, d'you know. Oh and there's many's the widow-woman knocking about, waiting to get in here. And what at all in the next world would I do if they put another woman down on top of him before me?

She smiles up at **Vera**. **Vera** *smiles.*

Mrs Conneeley (*straightens up*)   That's the way we are and what about it . . . Well?

Vera   Heigh-ho!

Mrs Conneeley (*her two hands on top of* **Vera**'s)   . . . You'll be all right.

Vera *leaves. The purr of the car and it drives off.* **Mrs Conneeley**'s *hand held up in a farewell. Now, her attention on the grave, (downstage side of it, her back to us) like someone preparing a bed.*